Semester Abroad:

A College Student's Guide to Europe

by
Kimberly Reid

authorHOUSE®

AuthorHouse™
1663 Liberty Drive, Suite 200
Bloomington, IN 47403
www.authorhouse.com
Phone: 1-800-839-8640

First published by AuthorHouse 12/12/2007

ISBN: 978-1-4343-3333-9 (sc)

*Printed in the United States of America
Bloomington, Indiana*

This book is printed on acid-free paper.

Dedicated to:

Brenda and David Reid for all of your help and support with this project. And to Lesely Mund, Kelly Turner, Rachel Stanley, and Rebecca Wynne for an incredible time abroad filled with stories and laughs.

Contents

Foreword

My sophomore year of college at Miami University in Oxford, Ohio proved to be the year that forever changed my life. I spent my first year and a half at Miami getting acquainted with college life, meeting new people, and as corny as it sounds, spreading my wings and gaining the independence and confidence that I needed. Many colleges and universities offer study abroad programs that allow students to take classes in different parts of the world for a semester while earning college credits. What sets Miami apart from most colleges is that in addition to the study abroad program, they also have an actual branch of Miami University housed in a chateau in the small European country of Luxembourg.

View from Miami University Campus in Luxembourg

Every semester approximately 150 students get the opportunity to live in Luxembourg and attend class in the chateau. Miami does not have dormitories in Luxembourg but instead finds housing with local residents for the students. The program enables students to take classes during the week and travel around Europe on the weekends. The semester I went, we also got an entire week off from classes for spring break and another week for Carnival. It was a truly incredible experience. I would be in class on Wednesday learning about an 11th Century painting and on Saturday I would be standing in front of the actual painting at the Uffizi in Florence, Italy.

During my four and a half months in Europe I visited twenty-one countries and nearly every major city. I did everything from tobogganing in Salzburg to sailing in Greece. While I was in Europe I was so busy enjoying myself that I did not take the time to keep a complete journal of my experiences, and upon arriving back to the States my fist thought was to log all of my travel experiences so that I would not forget one detail. Friends asked me for advice and tips because they were getting ready to spend a semester in "Lux." "What was your favorite city?" "How do the trains work?" "Did you have language problems?" "What kind of rail pass should I get?" I wrote down tips and suggestions for them that I picked up during my trip. I wrote about the countries I had been to and pointers that would be helpful. Next thing I knew, my writing had developed into more of a "how-to travel guide" for college students. I thought if it was helpful to my friends, maybe there were others that could benefit from it. While preparing for my trip I found that most of the travel books available are either for someone backpacking their way around Europe or for family vacations. There just wasn't a book for someone like me – a student traveling on the weekends with limited time and money. Many of the famous landmarks and no-brainer activities can be found in just about any of the typical travel books. I chose a different avenue; some suggestions of the best ways to tour cities and other tips geared for the young traveler. I was a student with limited finances and limited time to travel. This book is written from that perspective. I tell you what I think is the easiest way to see what each city has to offer. I hope all you need is this book and a map to lighten your backpack and give you the confidence to travel Europe.

I have only written on those cities and countries that I have visited. Everything you read comes from my own personal experiences and the lessons I learned while abroad. Hopefully these tips, suggestions, and stories can prepare you and enhance your travel experiences. Trust me when I say that I did not spend four and a half months in Europe without making a few mistakes, but hopefully with the help of those blunders and information I impart in this book, you will be able to avoid many of the same mistakes and be one step ahead.

Lastly, one thing that I found very helpful to appreciating and enjoying Europe, is knowing its history. Living in America, we think a building is old when it was built in 1820. We are a young country. In Europe, a building built in 1820 would not be considered anything overly special. Europeans talk in centuries not years when it comes to their landmarks and they are very proud of their history. The heritage of Europe's cities is so rich that at least having a brief overview of their history makes the experience much more enjoyable. The locals will also appreciate that you are not ignorant of their past. In each country's chapter, I have included a few paragraphs explaining the highlights of their history just to give a little background for when you are standing in front of a historical site or building. It helps to appreciate what you are viewing.

Before You Go

One thing that I found to be very important was to take the time to prepare for each trip. By this I just mean to find out what you need to take and what you can leave at home. My university was a very helpful and knowledgeable resource since they send 150 students to Europe every semester. Another invaluable aid is the U.S. Customs website (http://www.cbp.gov/xp/cgov/travel/vacation/). This website can answer many questions and provide updated information. *Before You Go* outlines some of the key tips I learned with information to help make your trip hassle-free. A checklist is also included at the back of this chapter.

Vaccinations and Inoculations

The Center for Disease Control and Prevention (CDC) provides information on the vaccines needed for travelers to destinations around the world. They separate the vaccines into three categories: routine, recommended and required. This information can be obtained from the CDC's website (http://www.cdc.gov/travel/vaccinat.htm). Ideally 4 to 6 weeks before your trip you should see your doctor for any needed vaccinations and inoculations.

Visas and Passports

With the growing number of people frequently traveling between the U.S. and Europe, it is fairly simple to leave on extended vacations without a problem. No visa is required unless you will be living there for over six months. I obtained a temporary visa for my four months in Luxembourg through the University because my new address was in Luxembourg. However, if you are just traveling and bouncing from city to city, no official visa is necessary.

Passports are necessary entering and exiting the continent and each country within. All airports have a check station. There are usually two lines to choose from: one for citizens of the European Union and one for the "Non-EU Residents;" clearly, Americans are "Non-EU Residents." It is extremely important that you keep your passport on you at all times. Your passport not only identifies you as an American and gives you some legal rights, but it is checked and rechecked. Every time you take the train the conductors ask to see your passport. The reason for this is because they compare it to the name on either the Eurail pass or the point-to-point ticket. Hotels and hostels refer to it also. Some places ask to keep your passport as a means for accountability and identification. Usually this is quite legitimate, but I never like to have my passport away from me, so I offered them another form of identification like a student ID or my U.S. Driver's License; often this was acceptable. Keeping track of your passport is critical to an enjoyable trip in Europe. Beware of pickpockets and thieves. Like everywhere else in the world, Europe does have its share of criminals. This is said not to scare or deter you from going, but to make you aware that it does happen. Don't be naïve and trusting with your passport, make sure to keep it secure. Most places are safe and the people are honest but it only takes one careless moment and one pickpocket to make your trip a disaster.

ISIC Card

An easy way to save some money is to exploit the fact that you are a student. College students get numerous discounts on museum entrance fees, plays, hostels, and sometimes on tours. The card costs around $25 and can only be obtained in the U.S.; it more than makes up for its cost with a few uses. Many places do not post that they accept the card or that it gives a discount, but simply make it a habit to ask. It will take a couple euros off here and a couple euros off there to ultimately save you a lot of money. By purchasing this card you are also purchasing a limited amount of travel insurance. In case you are injured or have been a victim of theft, this card will give some extra support to make claims. And finally, the ISIC card is yet another piece of identification. It never hurts to have an extra form to identify you. Keep this on you as well, it is not a hassle and it saves some much-needed cash.

Major Purchases Before You Go

Obviously, your first major purchase will be your round trip plane ticket to Europe. Depending on the time of year you will be traveling, there are quite a lot of good fares but the price of the ticket is higher when planning an extended stay. If you will be traveling around Europe, pick a city to fly in and out of that is convenient for your itinerary both at the beginning and at the end of your trip.

The next major purchase is a rail pass. To get around Europe, the best way is by train. The Eurail pass offers many different options as explained in the *Getting Around* chapter. The rail pass can only be purchased in the U.S., and once in Europe you can only purchase point-to-point tickets. Decide where you will be traveling, which pass is best for you, and then purchase it through a travel agent or online at www.Eurail.com. For my trip I purchased two different passes. For the first month I purchased a Benelux pass, which was good for travel in Belgium, The Netherlands and Luxembourg. Then for the remaining three months of my trip I had an unlimited pass for most of Europe. My thinking was that I would get acclimated to things the first few weeks by traveling closer to my Luxembourg home and then I would be ready to travel a little farther away. The key is to think about what you plan to do and buy the appropriate pass. If you do not plan to travel a lot while in Europe, you may want to just purchase point-to-point tickets when you get there.

Accommodations and tours generally do not need to be purchased far in advance. Hotels usually have a booking policy of a few days prior, but hostels can be booked online the night before if needed. If you will be staying in one place for the duration of your trip, having accommodations booked ahead of time is probably the wise decision. However, if you are backpacking or spontaneously changing destinations, hostels sometimes take walk-ins or bookings the night before (depending on high or low season and any major travel event in the area). I would definitely recommend having accommodations booked for the first night or two. You will be exhausted from your flight and the last thing you want to do is find a place to stay. This will also give you a little time to familiarize yourself with the area and figure out what you want to do next.

Deciding What to Take and Packing

Nobody looks forward to packing for a vacation. The hassle of determining what clothes to bring, what weather protective items to consider, and essential travel materials to remember is a tedious project that takes some time. The length of your stay and the destinations visited will directly influence packing. Functionality becomes primary while style becomes secondary. I would pack one or two pairs of pants with just a few sweaters. By finding clothes that I could layer or mix and match, I only needed three or four shirts to make outfits for a week and a half.

Investing money in a good pair of walking shoes is essential. Without noticing, many times you will walk ten miles in one day going from café to museum to city park. Ensure your shoes are comfortable and waterproof so that they can be used any time. As we all know, weather is unpredictable and can be the cause of many frustrations and delays. Being prepared for the weather will be a great help later. A small umbrella, waterproof shoes, and a weatherproof jacket will make traveling in the rain less of an issue. Carrying bags, cameras, umbrellas, and maps, makes a person start to feel like a pack mule. Condense as much as possible by putting bags inside of bags or waiting until right before returning to the hostel to stop by that store you liked. It keeps your hands free for an umbrella or to take an impromptu picture. With the sporadic rains of London, I quickly became tired of lugging around an umbrella so I put it into my backpack and used it only when the rain became too much for the hood of my jacket. Keep it light and easy.

Europeans typically have a much different fashion sense than Americans. It is true that they wear more neutral colors like blacks, browns, and grays and less jeans. I was warned that I would stick out like an American because of my tennis shoes, jeans and bright sweaters. Truth is: you are noticed to be an American before you even open your mouth. It is seen through our demeanor, our hair, our clothes, and even down to our walk. My only advice is to just tone back. Go ahead and wear your jeans or tennis shoes, but try to avoid flashy colors, American university sweatshirts or anything screaming American. You are a tourist and they expect you to wear the fashion of your home country, but the more you blend in, the less "touristy" you feel, enabling you to take in the city as if it were your own.

The one item that cannot be overlooked is a money pouch. They are advertised on travel documentaries or on tours, but they really are useful. There are options to get the ones that go around the waist or around the neck. Money pouches go under the clothes to be unseen and it makes it nearly impossible for personal affects to be stolen. This is where I kept my passport, Eurail pass, money, and credit cards. Carrying a purse or a wallet in the back pocket is a simple target for a career pickpocket to steal all of your valuables. Once you get over the "cool-factor" and initial hassle of it, it becomes quickly apparent how important this inexpensive travel essential really is. Keep only small amounts of money in your purse or pocket, generally an amount that will not hurt too much if lost or stolen. The rest should be kept in the money pouch or belt.

Something also easily forgotten is contact numbers and addresses. Either in your money pouch our in your bag, put the numbers and addresses down of family and friends back home or the place you are staying while in Europe. If you have an emergency, get lost, or simply need directions somewhere this makes it much simpler to contact someone. Many desk clerks at hotels and hostels speak English and are more than willing to help out with directions or any other assistance. Be sure to write down the numbers and locations of American embassies in each of the capitals. If for some reason there was a serious problem this would enable you to find help quickly. Lastly, numbers to the Eurail home office, your airline, and any other major ticketed purchases you have is useful. All of this information can be put onto one sheet of paper and go virtually unnoticed the entire time you are gone, but in the chance you need help, you will always have a way to reach someone.

Don't forget any entertainment you might need during the hustle and bustle of packing. You will spend some downtime either in the hostels or on trains and you might need a book or iPod to pass the time. If there was a particular book I wanted to read, I would buy a used copy at a half-price store in the U.S. and then when I was finished, I threw it away or left it in my hostel to lessen the weight of my bag and create more room for souvenirs I bought. Packing lightly and efficiently is crucial. Entire days walking through busy cities with heavy packs can quickly become exhausting. By being smart and practical while packing, you will reap the benefits of packing one less pair of jeans or that bulky knit sweater that takes up space.

Another thing to consider is the size of the backpack itself. Some fellow students brought the big hiking type backpacks. They soon came to regret that decision. Unless you plan to spend a lot of time backpacking outdoors, these are not advisable. Backpacks get pretty heavy when you carry it around a city all day. I bought a roomy backpack that was not much bigger than one used in school, but was still big enough to store clothes for a weekend trip. For my weeklong trips, I also had a small bag with a shoulder strap. This was generally plenty of room. I did buy a small nylon bag that would fold up to about the size of a wallet and kept it packed in case I bought too many souvenirs to fit in my backpack.

One other important item I found was a set of sleep sheets. They can be purchased at any sporting goods store and are nothing more than a thin lightweight fleece that resembles a sleeping bag with a zipper up the side. They roll up small and I attached mine to the bottom of my backpack in a little nylon bag along with a small pillow. These come in handy on long train rides. Also, some hostels charge an additional fee for sheets. Even if sheets were provided I usually felt more comfortable sleeping in my own sleep sheet.

The electrical current adapter is an essential item. It can be purchased at most stores that carry travel accessories. Different countries have different kinds of electrical outlets. The adaptors allow you to use your appliances such as blow dryers and chargers for cameras and iPods. The one I had was about 1"x1"x3" and it had the different adaptors that I needed for all 21 countries I visited.

One important thing to remember both on your way to Europe and on your way home is that there are baggage weight and size limits. The charges for oversized or overweight bags can be quite expensive. When I traveled to Europe in 2004 the airline limited checked baggage to 70 pounds for international flights. You can ask your airline or check their website for the current restrictions. I know on my return from Europe several of my fellow students were going through their bags at the airport and discarding clothing and personal items to get their baggage weight down.

Money

Exchange rates are best by using a credit card in Europe. Be sure to notify your card company if you will be spending a lot of time and money in Europe. If the card has not been used frequently and is suddenly being put towards hotels in Zurich, then the card company may temporarily freeze accounts to investigate the atypical usage. Avoid any problems like this by calling your credit card company before you leave to make them aware that you will be making such purchases. Also, be sure to take some Euros with you as well. Depending on how long you are staying, 250€ is a nice start for a two week period of liquid cash. When arriving in a foreign city after traveling for several hours the last thing you want to do is try and exchange money so that you can take a cab to your hotel. Taking some Euros with you will help until you get acclimated. Larger banks in most major U.S. cities will have plenty of Euros in stock, but for smaller cities notify your tellers that you will need to exchange Dollars for Euros. Sometimes it may take up to a week or two for them to get the Euros you need.

Make Copies

Before leaving, make two photocopies of your passport, Visa, ISIC card, plane ticket, rail pass and any other travel documents you feel are important. Leave one copy at home with your emergency contact and take one with you. Keep the copies you take with you separate from the actual hard copy of each, so in case your money pouch is stolen the copies hidden in your backpack or luggage are available to use when talking to police or embassy officials. In addition to these documents, you may also want to copy sales receipts of certain purchases that you made for your trip. Upon arriving back to the United States you will have to fill out a customs forms declaring the overseas purchases you are bringing back to the U.S. The limit is generally pretty high for a poor college student (at press time it is $800) so unless you are a big shopper, you will probably not exceed the duty-free limit. Copying receipts for items that may be mistaken as being purchased abroad – i.e. new cameras, Swiss watch, or jewelry will give you proof that they were purchased in the U.S. in case you are asked to declare them. Readily identified items with permanently affixed serial numbers or markings can also be taken to a customs office and registered before your departure. You will be given a certificate of registration to expedite free entry of those items back into the U.S.

Travel Books and Maps

Obviously, I think this book is a must take item. It can be a handy reference while you are away. Also, maps of major cities are available in most large bookstores. Maps can be purchased in Europe but sometimes they are not in English, which makes things a little difficult. If you do take a few maps, try to get *small*, detailed maps of the cities you plan to visit. It is difficult and frustrating to unfold a large map every time you want to quickly check a destination. A small book that has phrases in various languages is helpful if there are any major language barriers.

Packing Checklist

_____ This Book ☺

_____ Small maps of a few of the cities you will visit

_____ Passport and/or Visa

_____ ISIC Card (if you are a student)

_____ Eurail Pass

_____ Plane ticket

_____ Money Pouch to wear under clothing to protect money, passports, etc.

_____ Emergency Contact name, number and address

_____ Credit card company contact information in case of loss or theft.

_____ Euros

_____ Travelers checks

_____ Credit cards

_____ Copies of purchase receipts (if you have them) for items that may be mistaken as purchased abroad – i.e. cameras, Swiss watch, jewelry to prove that you brought the item from home, so you don't have to pay duty on it when returning home.)

_____ Photocopy of travel and important documents (passport, return flight ticket, credit card)

_____ Entertainment (there is a lot of down time on trains, have something to pass the time like an iPod with music, books to read)

_____ Day pack for short trips

_____ Ziploc bags

_____ Waterproof walking shoes

_____ Waterproof jacket

_____ Umbrella

_____ Cameras

_____ Sweaters

_____ Pants

_____ Lightweight jacket

_____ Nice outfit for the occasional dinner

_____ Plug adapter

_____ Sleep sheet and small pillow

_____ Hat, scarf and gloves (No matter what season it can get cold in the mountains.)

Things to Know While Traveling

Perhaps the most important part of traveling around Europe is to make plans before leaving one destination for the next. This does not mean to make a strict itinerary and to never divert from it, because that does not take into account missed trains, site closings, holidays, etc. Having a general idea what you want to see and do while in each city is imperative. Europe is rich both culturally and historically and each city is populated with hundreds of must-see sites. A good way to ensure that you will see or do everything that you want is to make a list.

Make a list of all the sites you want to see.

Each city has a completely different feel. You can walk through the countless number of Roman ruins in Italy or stroll through parks in London. Are you more interested in the historical aspects? Modern day architecture? The landscape? Or the cultural flair of each place? Write down all the places of interest that catch your attention so you are sure not to miss one. By making a preliminary list it promises that you won't absentmindedly forget an important site. It would be unfortunate if you spent all of the money and time to fly to a country and leave without seeing something that you may never get the chance to see again.

Check locations of site.

Any map or tour book probably has a primitive list or location of all the major sites in each city. Check out the locations of each so you can visit them while in the same vicinity. Some of these cities are much larger than you can imagine (Berlin is eight times the size of Paris!!) and walking aimlessly back and forth between places will not only become frustrating but wear you down by making you walk an unnecessary number of extra miles or go broke hiring cabs.

Check Times and Holidays.

In each chapter I list some of the major holidays in the countries and the normal working hours. This is important because Europeans love their time off of work and take advantage of it whenever possible. Note that many of the countries take

10

about a two hour lunch break in the middle of the day to spend time with familiy, so their restaurant or store might not be open. Most museums and historical sites will be open the majority of the week, but if you want to catch a certain café or a museum pay attention to the hours and days they are open.

Cyber Cafes

In this book I often mention Internet websites. Do not think that you have to lug your laptop around with you. On my trip I did have the advantage of Internet access and computers at my college's chateau in Luxembourg, but not to worry, there are cyber cafes all over Europe. Generally, one can walk right into a cyber café and sit down at a computer without any problems. The charges for Internet access vary from city to city and by the overall quality of the equipment. Expect to pay in time blocks, where you may pay 5€ for each set of fifteen minutes. Another alternative are ones that you log onto and the timer begins immediately. Upon completion of your Internet session, simply take the time code over to the attendant and they will charge accordingly. Paying for Internet access will start to add up. Look into hostels that offer Internet or at cafes that offer free access with a meal. This way you can get two of what you want for the price of one.

Currency

While many of the countries in the European Union use the Euro, there are still coins that are not accepted out of the home country. Make converting to different currencies minimal and as close to the estimated amount you anticipate to spend. Money is lost on every transaction, so keep exchanges to a minimum to save. You can go to the website www.xc.com to check up-to-date conversion rates. Below is a list of the members of the European Union as of press time.

Austria	Latvia
Belgium	Lithuania
Bulgaria	Luxembourg
Cyprus (Greek part)	Malta
Czech Republic	Netherlands
Denmark	Poland
Estonia	Portugal
Finland	Romania
France	Slovakia
Germany	Slovenia
Greece	Spain
Hungary	Sweden
Ireland	United Kingdom of Great Britain
Italy	and Northern Ireland

Of the countries in the European Union, some still have yet to adopt the Euro as its standard for currency. These countries include: Bulgaria, Cyprus, Czech

Republic, Denmark, Estonia, Hungary, Latvia, Lithuania, Malta, Poland, Romania, Slovakia, Sweden and the United Kingdom.

Estimate prices.

Europeans know that each year millions of tourists come to their countries with the intention of visiting the sites and spending money. Some museums and entrance fees are pricey, but going onto the Internet makes it easy to identify prices. There are many cyber cafés where you can have a leisurely break and do research on the Internet. A lot of museums across Europe are free to the public a certain day each month, and occasionally passes for multiple museums and landmarks are much cheaper than buying them all individually. Be thrifty but not cheap. Experience all you can experience without overspending and being exploited by those trying to make a few bucks. Being informed and educated while traveling is so important when you are trying to see Europe on a modest budget.

Put your interests first.

It was a shame to see some other students not doing some of the things they had wanted to. Money tended to be a factor and so did time. One of my professors told me, "It is much cheaper to spend the extra Euros now to do what you want, as opposed to later when you would have to fly back and see it." This is completely true. I would always ask myself, "Will I regret not doing this?" If I had even a shred of doubt, then I went ahead and did it. The memories more than make up for the money and if you plan right to begin with, you should already be within reason of your budget.

These are just a few no-brainers that will only add to the overall experience of your trip. I had spent many vacations with my parents, but I had never gone on a trip without them other than a week at spring break or a weekend trip with friends. Each weekend came with a new lesson that I learned. After walking 25 miles in Paris looking for the endless number of sites, I reevaluated my travel plans to make them more organized and beneficial to my friends and me. Leave the possibility open for a chance encounter or an unforeseen opportunity such as a London play. More amazing things happen when you are laid back and open to changes in the plan. Know what you want to see and do, but sometimes the best things are what you least expect.

Getting Around

One thing that Europe has done exceptionally well is implement the use of public transportation. It is simple to use and the best way to get around. Trains connect every major city with lines reaching even into small towns. Some lines offer high speed alternatives to get around in nearly half the time while others offer a more leisurely, panoramic view of the landscape outside. Whether going from country to country or street to street, Europe has the most effective and easy-to-use system to transport not only the familiarized locals, but tourists as well.

Eurail

If you are making an extended stay in Europe, there is no better way to get around than by using a Eurail pass. The pass can only be purchased in the United States through the website or a travel agent. By going to www.Eurail.com you can look up all of the different options.

> *flexi-pass
> *unlimited
> *selecti-pass

This was by far one of the most enjoyable parts of traveling. I could get from point A to point B and watch the Swiss Alps out my window. Some of the most serene and picturesque sights you will ever see will be included in the price and comfort of your Eurail pass.

Trains, Tickets, and Stations

For the most part, all of the routes in your determined Eurail pass are already paid for and no other payments need to be made. It is important that you check the boards or manuals at each of the train stations. If there is a notation next to your route, usually an exclamation point (!) then you must reserve a seat on that train. This can cost anywhere from 3€ to 25€. These routes are typically the most heavily demanded ones, for instance, Florence to Milan or Paris to Nice. If you do not pay this reservation fee, then the conductor when checking your ticket will fine you and it is usually double the reservation fee. These trains have a reservation requirement for a reason. I have been on trains before that were over booked and people sat in between the train cars or on the ground waiting for the next stop when people got off, freeing up a seat.

After making your reservation, the teller will give you a ticket that identifies your train number, car number, aisle and seat. It is very systematic and easy to find your seat once you are familiar with the process. First, check to see that you are getting on the train going to your destination. Often times the train splits into two smaller trains, each going in a separate direction. The final destination is usually labeled in each train car or with a sign on the outside door. Make sure to check the train car each time you board. Also, there may be multiple trains going in the same direction the only difference may be the stops or the times. Be sure to double check which train goes where and the actual train number. You do not want to be on one of two trains going to Barcelona, but the one you get on leaves later and does not stop at the stop you wanted.

Yet another hassle for travelers to consider when using the train system is that in most cities there are multiple stations. Typically there is the central station accompanied by a few subsidiary stations. The main station has more services and trains offered, and it is usually placed in a more central location in the city. The best way to avoid these problems is to check the train number to make sure it matches the route and schedule you want.

Second, find the car that is mentioned on your ticket. There are usually conductors on the platform or by the steps to help. They can point you in the correct direction or simply look at the numbers listed on the door to each car. Then, walk to the aisle and above the seats should be a piece of paper listing your name and which portion of the trip you will be sitting in that seat. This is because if you are getting off at a certain stop, someone who reserved a seat could have yours on the second leg of the trip. Double check that your name is on a sheet above your seat, if not, contact the conductor and he or she will make sure all is in order.

When reserving a seat tell the teller if you prefer a smoking or non-smoking car. The Europeans love their cigarettes and if you do not like the fog of dense smoke, then the smoking cars could be a little overpowering. Also, remember to mention that you would like a student, or second-class seat. This is much less expensive and not all that different from the first class seats.

One last important thing to mention when boarding a train is to check the door of the car you will be riding. If it is a train that did not require a reservation then it is possible that the train splits. On each of the doors of the train there is a sign indicating if that particular car is: smoking or non-smoking, second class or first class, reserved or not reserved, and its final destination. As long as the final city is farther down the tracks then where you are going, you will be fine.

The train system can seem overwhelming at times, but it is quite simple. There are a number of resources to use to find times and routes that will appeal to you. Online, www.bahnhafas.de gives just about every thing one needs to know about the trains. It will indicate what times the stops are, if there is a reservation needed, if the train splits, etc. You can log on to that site, enter where you are and where you want to go, it will reply with all of the possible trains to take, the number of connections, times, and stops. This became a staple in my traveling and I used it several times daily. Eurail puts out a book that lists all of the routes it offers, the stops, times, and reservation requirements as well. This may be a good resource to keep in your bag when spontaneously deciding to change plans. If all else fails go to the train station itself. Times and destinations are listed on bulletins located throughout every train station. Big boards are set as the focal point in the center of the station for the trains first to depart. There are always workers available to answer any questions or concerns that you might have. Many speak English or have devised ways to bridge the communication gap. Train stations are usually toward the center of town and are a spectacle of tons of people coming and going from places all over Europe. I assure you that you will not be the only tourist there. Be open to asking questions and asking for help. It will only take one or two times before you become proficient in the European train system.

City Transportation

Every city in Europe has a well-established transportation system. Hearing the words "public transportation" may seem a little daunting by comparing it to what we have in the States; however, Europe's public transportation is extremely prompt, safe, and clean. Subways are by far the easiest way to get around. Stops are located all over the city with steps that lead down under the streets and take people to the trains that make it throughout some of the busiest cities in the world without traffic. Tickets need to be purchased before getting on the metro (subway) or else you will not make it through the turnstiles. There are booths right before the turnstiles leading to the metro. In most cases you will not need to know the exact stop you are getting off at, instead you just need to purchase a ticket. The prices vary from city to city, but they are generally around 1,50€. Knowing a plan will help when deciding how many tickets to purchase. If you will be using a lot of tickets for the metro or busses, you can purchase a packet of them or 24-hour passes. A denomination of 5, 10, or 20 is better economically and easier because you can avoid the hassles of a line. In most cities these tickets are good for the metro, buses, and trams. After sliding the ticket through the turnstile it is no longer valid. Hold on to your stamped ticket, because sometimes conductors on the metros will check them to make sure you are a paying customer. The fines for no ticket on metros and buses are very high and not worth the 1,50€ you would spend on the ticket itself.

Buses and trams sometimes have machines at the stops to purchases tickets. If they do not and you do not have a prepaid ticket, you can buy one on the bus from the driver or at a machine located on the bus. The honor system is used the majority of the time, but it is important that people maintain this honesty because it pays for the services provided by each country.

Routes can be confusing at times to decipher, but if you know where you are and where you want to go, the stops are easily labeled. Each bus, tram, metro stop, or route is clearly marked with boards showing all of the information. Find the stop you wish to go to, and walk in the direction of that board. Once you get on the transportation, watch the stops that go by until the one you want is next. With a little attention and using common sense, it does not take a lot to figure out the routes.

Rentals

In many countries students can rent cars and use them as means to see the country. You can get an international driver's license in the States, which makes it easier to obtain a rental. Most times auto insurance does not cover you in other countries; you may want to check with your insurance company before leaving. European cities are in a sense, organized chaos when it comes to driving. I would not recommend driving in any city unless you feel very comfortable and your insurance covers it. Traffic is outrageous and so are the speedy locals.

Bikes are another possibility. Countries like The Netherlands push for citizens and tourists to use the abundance of bikes. There are bike racks located all over the city and it is a cheap and easy way to see the sites while getting around a little bit quicker.

Taxis

It seems like taxis outnumber the people in Europe. They are everywhere and the drivers are extremely knowledgeable of their cities. Taxis are a good way to get around, but typically more expensive and sometimes not all of the drivers have the best of intentions. Make sure to set up a price before leaving or that they have a working meter attached to their car. Many times drivers take advantage of naïve tourists and take them on a ride that can cost a pretty penny. As long as you are aware and upfront, a taxi is a great way to get around a busy city.

Air

One last option is taking a plane. There are great deals to fly all over Europe and discount airlines that can get tourists to and from cities for modest prices and within only a couple of hours. Virgin Express (www.virginexpress.com) is a very reliable and inexpensive means to fly throughout Europe. It has desks in most of the major cities' airports.

A secret wonder is Ryan Air (www.ryanair.com). You can fly basically anywhere from 1€-50€ each way. No, I'm not lying. With the transfer fees and taxes added in, the prices are still exceptionally low. I flew from Frankfurt, Germany to Stockholm, Sweden for 25€. This cheap flight does come at a bit of an inconvenience though. The reason why these tickets are so cheap is because Ryan Air does not have terminals inside many of the major airports, they occupy secondary airports in outside towns. It might take a bus or an extra train to get to and from these airports, but many times it's more than worth it.

Accommodations

One of the most tedious and frustrating parts of traveling is finding accommodations for each night you spend out. There are a variety of different options to choose from and a lot of different factors to consider. The spontaneity of backpacking poses more of a problem than longer-term destinations. The European countries understand that they must cater to the independent travelers and generally make it easy for the backpacker to book rooms on short notice.

First you must consider the type of establishment at which you want to stay. Bed and Breakfasts are common in Great Britain and Ireland. These family-run, cozy places to sleep usually run in the middle of the pricing spectrum. Meals are sometimes included and mingling with the other guests is encouraged. B & Bs are a great way to step out and feel as though you are part of a welcoming family.

On the highest end of the prices are hotels. For the college-aged traveler, these accommodations are more expensive than they are worth. I opted to save more of my money to use on activities than where I was staying for the night. The majority of hotels do ensure daily cleaning services and other accommodations for the guest. One thing to consider in the decision is that if you are traveling in a larger group, sometimes hotels end up being cheaper than hostels. Hostels charge by the person and hotels charge by the room. Just do the math and figure which is better for your needs. There are other forms that hotels can take on. Places like Stockholm and Prague have what are called botels. These are boats that have been turned into hotels. They sit on inlets or in the river, swaying to the natural motions of the water. To mix it up a little, botels are fun and interesting ways to change the typical night of sleep into an experience.

Hostels are the person on a budget's dream. For the price of a nice dinner, you can stay in a communal room for the night with other travelers just like you. Depending on how large the hostel and the city where it is located, the size of the room may vary. I traveled in groups of five and it was almost always just us in a room, so the fear of the unknown roommates was nearly nonexistent. However, meeting others on the same adventure as you is not the worst thing. When we did room with strangers from around the world, we would often stay up late and talk with them about our homes or trade advice on where the best places were to eat or visit. Hostels are a fantastic way to get tourist information and to learn more about different places. There is the risk of theft, though, because you do not have a private room you can lock. Most of the time I felt quite safe with the others around, but there is always a sense of insecurity that can make you slightly nervous. Check before getting a room if there are lockers. Often times there is a slight 2€ fee, but the peace of mind is worth it.

Hostels have a lot more that need to be researched about them before staying for the night. Websites like www.hostels.com and www.hostelseurope.com are great pages to research hostels and to book online. Check for lockers, clean sheets, how many per room, if a meal is included, Internet connections, and if there is a curfew. Don't be surprised to find that some hostels have curfews. Since there is a bunch of different people staying in the same building, the owners like to make it a courtesy to the others. If you are the type to stay out late, make sure not to book a hostel that has a curfew. Hostels are everywhere in Europe and usually open to last minute reservations or walk-ins, but if you know you are going to be staying in the same city for a few days, do your best to book early to ensure that you have a room for your length of stay.

Two other options are convents and sleep-ins. Many old convents that used to house monks and nuns have been turned into accommodations for travelers. Usually in a beautiful historic district, these convents are well priced, always clean, and have great service. Check while in places like Italy for these types of stays and vary your traveling experiences. Also there is what are called sleep-ins. These are basically large open rooms with a great expanse of space for travelers to stake their claim on a piece of floor and sleep there for the evening. Sleep-ins are by far the cheapest places to stay in Europe, but you give up a lot comfort, privacy and security for saving a little bit of money.

As you can see, there are a lot of different options to a good night's sleep in Europe. Many factors have to be weighed, from budget to privacy to meeting new people. Each accommodation gives you a different type of experience and one that I'm sure will be catalogued in your memory bank of Europe.

Etiquette

Perhaps one of the most important sections of this book for me is focusing on etiquette and how to appreciate the local cultures. Nothing infuriated me more than seeing U.S. tourists acting like the "ugly American" as many of the Europeans describe it. There is a distinct difference between our culture and that of the Europeans and by becoming visitors to their countries we need to embrace and respect their ways of life.

During the time I spent with European families and professors the topic of American tourists came up quite often. Overwhelmingly their biggest complaint was the way Americans interacted with one another. In the States we tend to talk louder and stand farther away from one another. In Europe, conversations are held at a more hushed tone and are less disruptive. In one discussion I had a man said, "It's almost like the Americans feel that their conversation is so important that we care to hear what they talk about. It is rude and disrespectful to all that are sitting around them." Please be mindful of this and keep conversations at a lower tone in order to avoid offending the locals.

Do not underestimate

Many Americans have not learned or taken the time to learn a foreign language. This is not the case in Europe however. Nearly all know at least two sometimes even five or six languages. Because of the close proximity to other countries and languages it becomes necessary for them to learn and develop a prowess in other languages. It has happened one too many times that an American tourist was in a conversation with another American discussing their distaste for the French culture or that Dutch lady's shoes. We must remember that an overwhelming majority of Europeans speak English quite well (some even better than us) and can fully understand what is being said. I am on a personal mission for Europe and its citizens to stop encountering these U.S. tourists that give the rest of us a bad name. Respecting and embracing other cultures only enhances time spent in those countries and sometimes gives an unexpected and enjoyable conversation with a local.

Dining

This part of traveling in Europe seems to be one of the hardest areas for American tourists to adjust. Europeans love fine cuisine and take their time with lunches and dinners to talk about politics or just to catch up. Few Europeans eat breakfast at a restaurant; instead they grab a pastry or cup of coffee and enjoy reading the daily news in the paper. Breakfasts consist of breads or cheeses and tend to be very light. After the first part of the work day ends, a couple hour siesta gives some time to reenergize for the rest of the day. The small breakfast and extended break gives Europeans the time to generally participate in a large lunch. Lunch is their largest meal of the day and can sometimes include multiple courses. There is usually a salad, soup, appetizer, entrée, cheese, and dessert, and it sometimes lasts for a couple of hours. Living in a society of drive-thrus and scarfing down Big Macs®, it is a nice change of pace to relax and have a long meal at lunch. Many restaurants in the United States keep the room temperature fairly low and encourage fast meals to ensure a quick table turn and thus increase their profit. Dining is looked at completely the opposite way in Europe. The server will not continually come over to check if your meal is to your satisfaction. They believe in letting you enjoy your meal without the interruptions and if you need something, you will ask. In Europe, do not feel rude by calling over your server for more bottled water or the check.

The ambiance of European restaurants is hard to match in the U.S. Tables are either stretched along a promenade outside on the patio or inside in a cozy, candlelit room. The temperature is comfortable and the atmosphere is eerily quiet. Once again, Europeans like to keep their conversations to themselves and to participate in a more relaxed atmosphere. Don't feel forced to whisper, but more importantly be aware of those around you. It took the first few times to feel comfortable with the quiet atmosphere, but upon returning to the U.S. I would have given anything to go back to the relaxing, peaceful meals that I experienced while abroad.

Dinners begin later and on a smaller scale in Europe. After a large lunch around 2 o'clock, dinner starts anywhere from 7 to 9. Some families choose to make dinners at home but the restaurants are still crowded with those looking for an effortless meal. It is important to note that serving in Europe is a respected profession. In the U.S., many of the servers you see will be under 30 and paying off loans or feeding a shopping problem (that's me!). The demographics are much different abroad. Most of the servers are in or well past their thirties and have been in the profession for years. It is an opportunity to climb the ranks and become the best server in that particular restaurant. Servers are paid a salary and do not earn the majority of their income from tips. It is not expected to give a tip after paying for the meal, but each country differs in its protocol for tipping. There are taxes and already implemented salaries to pay for the service of your server. However, this is not to say that tips are not welcomed. Typically, it is not common to leave paper bills, rather leave loose coins. In Euros, some of the denominations are 1€ or 2€, which will be the equivalent to two or three dollars.

Clothing

As I discussed earlier, I do not feel that we must hide whom we are in order to "fit in." As I approached people they automatically began speaking to me in English because it was vividly apparent by my jeans and t-shirts that I was an American. Many Europeans told me that they could identify Americans not only in the different clothing fashions or hairstyles but also by they way we walked and talked. They told me we have a type of "swagger" that is identifiable. I liked to think that in no way was I able to obtain a swagger from living in Cincinnati my whole life, but they assured me I could be pegged as an American from a mile away. For these reasons, there is no need to be ashamed or apprehensive to be labeled American, but there are a couple of ways to not over-do it. Try not to wear anything with American universities, sports teams or name brands sprawling across the front of the chest. There are some who make a living by preying on unsuspecting Americans and this walking advertisement is silly. There is no reason to advertise more American qualities than necessary. With political differences and a history of setting ourselves apart, some have not completely warmed up to Americans infiltrating their streets and taking snap shots of the their historic sites. Try your best to fit in and become a part of the European culture while traveling abroad. Show a respect for their culture by trying to blend in rather than disregarding it and showing arrogance.

Conversations

It is inevitable that at some point you will need to speak to a local. However intimidating this may seem, I encourage it. An overwhelming majority of Europeans speak English, whether fluently or conversationally, and can answer your questions without a problem. Usually owners or employees at hotels, hostels, and transportation services speak English and can help you, however; these people were not readily available on the back streets of Prague when I was lost at 2 in the morning. If you have a few minutes before leaving for your trip, attempt to learn some key phrases in the host language. Type them up on a sheet of paper if necessary to use as a tool to show the people. French, German, and Spanish may be a lot easier to master key phrases like, Pardon monsieur, Guten Tag, or Hola. Attempt to speak in their language first when approaching for help. After nine years of taking French I was fairly confident in my abilities to communicate my questions. I would say in French "Excuse me, where is the Notre Dame Cathedral?" and they would respond in English by saying, "Down the hill, to the right." It appeared that my French accent was not as convincing as my overpowering English background. I know that you may not be proficient in a European language but I saw many people approach someone by automatically speaking English. Many Europeans see this as a conceited assumption that they should already know English. By saying, "Hello, do you speak English," in their language, many locals were more than willing to help. Key phrases like, Hello, Good-bye, Thank you, and Do you speak English, will help you tremendously.

The Best of List

Best nightlife.. Amsterdam, the Netherlands

Best place for a home base .... Luxembourg

Best place to hang with locals .... Dublin, Ireland

Best museums .... Paris, France

Best place to eat at a cafe.............................. Italy

Best shopping.. Florence, Italy

Best place to take a guided tour..................... Scotland and Salzburg, Austria

Best river cruise .... London, The River Thames

Best weekend excursion .... South of Spain/Portugal/Morocco

Best wine tasting... Bordeaux, France

Best place to experience history.................... Rome, Italy

Best place to be touched by history............... Auschwitz, Poland

Best small town, quaint European city.......... Brugge, Belgium

Best landscape and outdoor activities .... Switzerland

Best public transportation system.................. Country – Germany, City - Paris

Best local cuisine .... Greece

Best place to meet other college students...... Prague, Czech Republic

Best place to get lost .... Scotland

Best place for pampering............................... Budapest, Hungary

Best beer .... Belgium

Best public squares .... Madrid, Spain

Best hostels .... Austria

Best value.. Poland

Best place for a picnic .... Corsica

Best beaches.. Greek Isles

Best castles.. Germany

Best changing of the guard .... Stockholm, Sweden

Best kept secret .... Krakow, Poland

Best atmosphere.. Oslo, Norway

Best desserts.. France

Best restaurants .... Belgium

Best place for souvenirs................................. Venice, Italy

Best place to snap a photo .... Switzerland

Austria

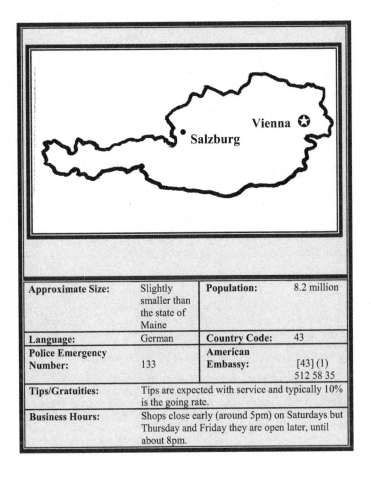

Approximate Size:	Slightly smaller than the state of Maine	Population:	8.2 million
Language:	German	Country Code:	43
Police Emergency Number:	133	American Embassy:	[43] (1) 512 58 35
Tips/Gratuities:	Tips are expected with service and typically 10% is the going rate.		
Business Hours:	Shops close early (around 5pm) on Saturdays but Thursday and Friday they are open later, until about 8pm.		

History and Overview:

Austria is a vibrant country with a rich and powerful past that has transcended history. One word comes to mind when thinking of Austrian history, the Hapsburgs. Although originally inhabited by Germanic tribes, the Hapsburg family gained power in the 14th and 15th centuries and started to impose their own thoughts upon the people. Catholicism was strictly enforced and citizens were encouraged to be devout. Austria today still follows a strong Catholic faith. During this time a good number of magnificent buildings were built in the Baroque style with ornate scrolls and curves. Many of these buildings still stand and show the extravagance and power of the Hapsburg family.

The Hapsburgs went on to marry into other royal families and added to their already large land holdings. The original Germanic tribes instilled a sense of the German way of life and the Germanic language. This stuck through the centuries and the Austrians still maintain a predominantly German culture. Rolling terrain has caused each of the different regions of Austria to have their own unique dress, dialect and daily traditions. That is why visiting the cities in the West by the Alps, is much different than the most important financial, political, and historic city of Vienna.

Places to Visit:

Austria is a land of beautiful architecture, picturesque landscape and an air of sophistication that gives it an all-together different feel than most other European countries. I found the people to be a little more stand-offish and the country to be more expensive and elegant than originally expected. Most tourists go straight for Vienna, but there are other popular tourist destinations that are less crowded and give a more down-to-earth feeling to Austria.

Salzburg

Salzburg is the land of Mozart and "The Sound of Music." This quaint town is dominated by a towering fortress in the city centre and the Salzach River that separates the old part of town from the new part of town. One can tour the city in a day or a long afternoon. Fewer crowds flock to Salzburg; but there is still enough tourism to keep visitors occupied and feeling catered to.

The western Austrian town gives its claim to fame as the birthplace and childhood home of Wolfgang Amadeus Mozart. You can stroll the streets to find Mozart's first home and other landmarks proudly displaying their connection to the famous composer. Souvenirs from small chocolate candies, to musical paraphernalia, to stuffed Mozarts are more than abundant. Salzburg's interest with its boy genius is just another reason for locals to be proud of their city. Salzburg is a great place to visit and a welcomed break from the bustling cities.

Aside from Mozart, Salzburg is famous for its connection with the classic musical, "Sound of Music" and the real life Von Trapp family. Embarrassed, though not ashamed, I am a huge fan of the movie and I hoped to visit Salzburg and the SOM Tour once I arrived in Austria. Even if you are not familiar or even dislike the movie the tour is probably the best way to get a guided tour of

House from The Sound of Music – Salzburg, Austria

Salzburg and the surrounding areas for a relatively inexpensive price. The tickets can be purchased at most hostels and tourist information offices at close to 30€ per person. The tour bus picks up guests at each of the hostels and gives a day-long trip showing the familiar sites of the "Sound of Music." Highlights are the Von Trapp house; the sprawling gardens where they sing "Do Re Me," and the gazebo. Not only are the movie sites shown, but the tour also takes you into the lake district of Austria, which is one of the more beautiful areas of the country. The lakes, the Austrian Alps, and small towns pass by as the bus continues on its way. If weather permits, there is even a stop to go tobogganing down the side of a mountain for nearly three minutes. Regardless of one's inclination to relive the "Sound of Music," this tour comes highly recommended and gives you the opportunity to see some of the best sites in Austria for a good price.

Whether a classical music fan or not, Salzburg is a great stop for many tourists in an otherwise chaotic European trip. It is relaxing, quaint and is supported by great sites of an old European town, sprawling countryside, and the chance to live like a kid again singing along to "Do Re Me."

Vienna

For a much different feel and a look at one of the most beautiful cities in Europe, many make Vienna a must-see on their list. Vienna is primarily known for its Vienna Boys Choir, the Opera and its shopping. There are more picture-worthy buildings and places to tour than can possibly be mentioned, so the best advice is to make a list of priorities. Like most European cities, in older times the city was surrounded and protected by a large stone wall, this is no different for Vienna. However, when the city outgrew the walls it was torn down and a transportation system known as the "Ring" was set up in its place. The easiest way to get a feel for the city is to hop on the Ring and to ride it around until you return to your original location. Almost all of the buildings are visible from the tram and it is then easier to gauge distances, proximity and the desire to see certain places. All of the tourist offices have brochures indicating the historical buildings and to make it easier on the tourist, each building has a number on them that directly corresponds to those brochures. Proper identification for each building is a breeze.

Inside the ring is the pedestrian friendly shopping district of Vienna. As far as the eye can see there are high-end stores and immense amounts of people like you, either perusing the boutiques or simply people-watching the thousands of diverse people along the pedestrian streets. The shopping, as well as everything else in Vienna is quite expensive. The locals seem to always be dressed in the finest clothes and the town screams class and sophistication. At times it was slightly intimidating, but remember, you are not the first or the last tourist on a budget to visit their city.

Inside the shopping district and located in the center of the Ring is St. Stephen's Cathedral. It can not be overlooked with its gold plated roof and dominating view in the centre square. Many street performers and protest demonstrations are located in this area. While I was there, there was a large demonstration for the legalization of marijuana which made it quite difficult to navigate around the crowd.

One nuisance you are bound to run into are men dressed as Mozart that are attempting to sell opera tickets and other performances by the famed composer. The solicitors target tourists and in effect, the show tends to lose its authenticity.

For a cheap and better alternative try for standing room tickets at the Vienna Opera. Probably the most famous and acclaimed opera in Europe, it is possible to get standing room tickets for less than 5€ a person. Contact the box office, entertainment offices, or tourist information offices to acquire tickets. Vienna Boys Choir tickets are much more expensive and along with the Opera, both are on vacation in July and August.

Spring is a great time to visit Vienna. The city does a wonderful job of maintaining the landscape and planting beautiful, colorful flowers throughout the capital. This makes the Palace, National Art Museum and nearby parks a pleasure to walk through the gardens and maybe even have a cheap and peaceful picnic along the way. After visiting many of the sites in Vienna, there is Shoengrin Palace just outside of the city centre where the Hapsburgs spent their winters. The crowd is huge and the tour is expensive. To see more regarding the lives of the empirical rulers, this is another stop to make while in Austria's capital if you are willing to tolerate the lines.

Vienna is an expensive city, but there are ways to save on some much needed spending cash. Look for inexpensive entertainment. Tours inside the palaces and other buildings can add up, so a few extra saved Euros can help. Identify what is most important to you. It may sound slightly cynical, but after a while palaces become less and less like a novelty and more like the norm. Pick and chose the ones you'd like to see and bypass the less interesting.

Stay in a hostel outside the Ring. In some cities a one star hotel or a bed and breakfast can be the same amount as a hostel and still remain at a very reasonable price; however, Vienna is not one of those cities. The farther you are away from the Ring, the cheaper the accommodations. European public transportation is phenomenal and it may only take another five minutes via the metro to get into town. I managed to find a hostel eight blocks from the train station and ten minutes into the shopping district for about 15€ a night. Also, you can purchase unlimited 24-hour tram/metro tickets for just 10€ that permits your travel on the Ring or any other transportation system for what just two one-way tickets might cost you.

Meals are what add up the most. Spending 10€ here and 10€ there quickly drains your bank account and puts those pastries right on your thighs. By going to a local grocery store you and whomever you are traveling with can split a loaf of bread, some deli meat and drinks for less than what it would cost for one of you to sip a coffee and nibble on a slice of cake from one of the famous Viennese coffee shops. This not only saves money, but also gives you more time to experience the locals and to take in the beautiful surroundings.

Austria's landscape and people give it a distinctly different feel than most of the other European countries. It cannot be missed and it provides tourists with the quintessential sophistication and class that many hope to see while visiting Europe. The people are interesting, the architecture is awe-inspiring and the landscape is better than what you might have imagined or seen in books. Austria provides both big-city luxuries and the small town surprises.

National Holidays	
January 1	New Year's Day
January 6	Epiphany
March/April	Easter Monday
May 1	Labor Day
May	Ascension Day
May/June	Pentecost Monday
May/June	Corpus Christi
August 15	Assumption of the Virgin
October 26	National Day
November 1	All Saints' Day
December 8	Immaculate Conception
December 25	Christmas Day
December 26	St. Stephen's Day

Belgium

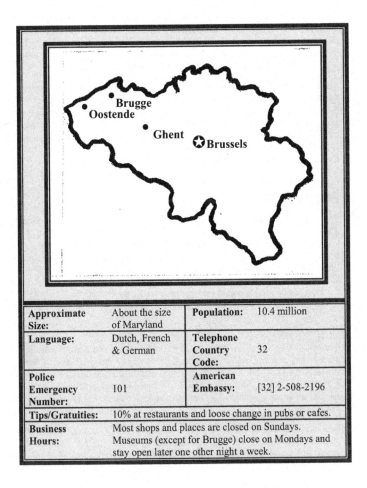

Approximate Size:	About the size of Maryland	Population:	10.4 million
Language:	Dutch, French & German	Telephone Country Code:	32
Police Emergency Number:	101	American Embassy:	[32] 2-508-2196
Tips/Gratuities:	10% at restaurants and loose change in pubs or cafes.		
Business Hours:	Most shops and places are closed on Sundays. Museums (except for Brugge) close on Mondays and stay open later one other night a week.		

History and Overview:

The low-land country of Belgium has fought through many decades of invasion and separation. Originally occupied by a Celtic tribe, the Germanic tribes eventually pushed their way into the Northern parts of present-day Belgium. After tumultuous encounters with Attila the Hun around 300 a.d., the Celts were forced to move across the North Sea to Britain and Ireland. A century later the Franks invaded southern Belgium and settled down. This division between the German people to the north and Frankish to the south saw no compromise and the people lived freely and independently from one another. The separation in cultures and languages is most clearly seen in modern times through the language line running across the center of Belgium and creating the different cultures of the two areas. People on one side call French their native language while people on the other consider Flemish their native language.

The Hapsburg's Empire expanded as far north as Belgium and through marriage, the Dukes of Burghandy from Spain took control. This occupation by the Spanish and Austrians influenced the people of Belgium, but also made it quite prosperous. During this time major cities sprung up and Belgium became an important place for trade, art, and industry. This vital and dual-cultured country is now home to some of the most significant international buildings like the European Union (EU) Headquarters.

Places to Visit:

Belgium is one country in Europe that does not get the recognition it deserves. Through its geography and history it has become diverse with its mixture of both French and German ways. Many think it has the culinary expertise of the French chefs but the portions and well-rounded foods of Germany. Winemaking from France and beer brewing from Germany gives this country even more of which to be proud. Some of the best beers in the world come from Belgium and one of the most popular foods comes from there as well...the French fry.

Brussels

Brussels is the capital and center of the country, but in my opinion not the best place to experience Belgium. Although the language line goes directly through Brussels, most business and everyday conversations are held in French. Many organizations dealing in European affairs are also located in Belgium and if you are into the inner workings of government and international firms, Brussels is the place to see.

Brussels does not provide visitors with much to do other than to take a leisurely afternoon visiting the town square, marveling at the Art Nouveau of Victor Horta, and one of Brussels renowned museums. In the city centre is the fountain known as le Petite Jepin. Basically, it is a statue of a little boy with his hands on his hips proudly relieving himself, which conveniently becomes a fountain.

Ghent

About an hour and a half north of Brussels is the town of Ghent. It is famous for multiple treaties ending the War of 1812 and other altercations as well as the Ghent Altarpiece. To get from the train station to the center of town, it is easiest and quickest to take one of the trams. There are multiple lines that run straight into the city, but there are also some that merely loop the city (which is clearly the one I got on) and all you can hope to do is look out the window to see the city centre in the distance. After you get off in the center of town the best thing to do is walk around. There is not a whole lot to do in Ghent but walking the streets was just as enjoyable as paying admissions to take tours.

In an open square is the Cathedral of Saint Bavon which houses the Ghent Altarpiece. The inside of the church is breathtaking. There are exact replicas of the altarpiece and a lot of alcoves to view other pieces of art. Commentaries are given by a historian, usually in Flemish or French, to explain the history of the cathedral or a piece in that particular room. The altarpiece can be viewed in a separate room for a fee. If it does not mean that much to you the free replica can still give a great sense of the profundity of the piece.

After walking throughout the city we stumbled upon the Ghent Fortress. It is a medieval fortress with everything typical of old European Castles. Using my ISIC card I got a discount and took some time to walk through the centuries old castle. Each room has a plaque describing the functions of that particular space and interesting tidbits that make touring more fun. Headsets can also be purchased for a self-guided tour detailing each high point. Also in each room are medieval weapons and some knight suits. In the basement is a torture museum where you can note just how cruel life was back in those days. The fortress and the museum are extremely interesting and worth the entrance fee, but the view from the top was worth the admission alone. You can get a sprawling view of the city of Ghent and look at all of the red slanted roofs and architecture. I found the time sitting atop the fortress by myself looking at the beautiful city of Ghent was well worth the trip.

Brugge

The first weekend trip I was able to take while living in Luxembourg was to the town of Brugge in northern Belgium. It was a spontaneous decision and I had no preconceived notions of what to expect. Booking our hostel late and realizing there were no vacancies within a five-hour radius of us in Germany, France, or southern Belgium, my friends and I looked on the map and saw a dot that said Brugge. I had heard it was famous for its lace, but I had no other expectations or knowledge of the town.

The people of Brugge are extremely friendly and helpful. After booking our hostel through an Internet site we contacted the owner to solidify directions. Our train did not arrive until 1 o'clock in the morning and the owner offered to meet us at the train station and walk us to the hostel so that we would not get lost.

Throughout our visit any questions we had or any sign of confusion, a local was able and willing to help us with whatever we needed.

All of the streets are cobble-stoned and winding between centuries old buildings. It is the epitome of an old town, but still modern enough to accommodate any needs. Brugge is called "the Venice of the North" because of its many canals that weave throughout the city. There are panoramic boat rides on the canals showing the sites but walking along them through the windy streets and bridges gives a more local and less touristy feel.

Ask anyone in Brugge what to buy as a souvenir and he or she will say Brugge lace or its world-famous chocolate. A lace or chocolate shop is located about every ten feet (which may have contributed to my weight gain while in Europe). There are still schools where women go to train in the art of lace making and some of the pieces sold in shops go for thousands of Euros each. Smaller and more affordable pieces are abundant and easy to purchase.

After walking through the pedestrian cobble-stoned streets, we eventually ended up in the town square at the center of Brugge. There are different types of façades and colors surrounding the open public space. Inside this square are more shops and cafes lining the open area. These cafes, restaurants, and shops are typically the most expensive in the city and supply many of the same items sold along the outer streets. Side streets and family run shops are plentiful and easier on the budget.

The dominating site in the town square is the belfry towering over the other buildings and vendors on the street. It is free to climb to the first level of the building, but in order to go to the top by the bell a fee is required. The climb is quite crowded as the steps are narrow and as it is one of the main tourist attractions in Brugge. The ISIC card will again give you a discount but the decision has to be weighed if it is worth the hour or so to climb and the crowd you have to deal with.

Finally, another major spot to hit is one of Brugge's many breweries. The German influence on beer making has been adopted and improved by the Belgians. In most cases the price of admission includes a tour of the brewery and samples of the beer. It is a good way to spend a couple hours and learn more about the Belgian way of life and culture.

Oostende

A sleepy town lying on the edge of the North Sea and only a quick 30-minute train ride from Brugge is the city of Oostende. Immediately after stepping off the train the aroma of salt water and fish markets cloud the senses. Walk the main drag along the shore line, experiencing chaotic traffic and an open-air fish market leading to the beach and eventually to the North Sea. Just for mere pride and a story to tell, my friends and I took off our shoes and walked through the gritty sand to the waves of the water. After sticking my foot in the freezing cold of the January water I had had enough and put my shoes back on.

There is little to do in Oostende other than to walk the streets, visit the town's cathedral and to take a bitter cold dip in the North Sea. A quick couple of hours and a cheap train ticket gave me the opportunity to visit yet another place many can never say they have visited, and to see yet another town with its own individual character and identity.

National Holidays	
January 1	New Year's Day
March/April	Easter Monday
May 1	Labor Day
May	Ascension Day
May/June	Pentecost Monday
July 21	National Day
August 15	Assumption of the Virgin
October 26	National Day
November 1	All Saints' Day
November 11	Armistice Day
December 25	Christmas Day

Czech Republic

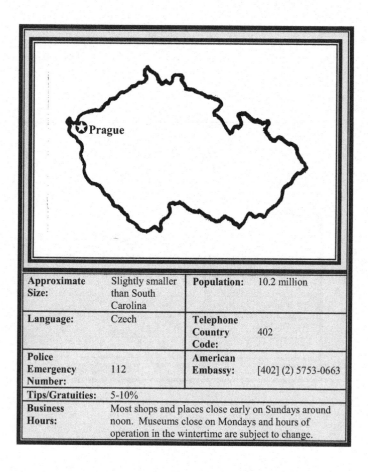

Approximate Size:	Slightly smaller than South Carolina	Population:	10.2 million
Language:	Czech	Telephone Country Code:	402
Police Emergency Number:	112	American Embassy:	[402] (2) 5753-0663
Tips/Gratuities:	5-10%		
Business Hours:	Most shops and places close early on Sundays around noon. Museums close on Mondays and hours of operation in the wintertime are subject to change.		

History and Overview:

Most Czech history starts after 1989 when Communism fell and the Czech Republic began to establish itself. Experiencing four centuries of Hapsburg rule and two world wars, it is a wonder how the Czech Republic has managed to stay beautiful and resilient. It is for this reason that Hitler made orders to ensure that Prague was the only major European city not to be bombed during World War II.

At the end of World War II, President Woodrow Wilson encouraged the country of Czechoslovakia to be formed. This would unite the two very different people of the Czechs and the Slovaks. Although the two groups were unique from each other they still bonded together to form a unified nation until they could recover from the wars. It wasn't until January 1, 1993 that the two countries split, forming the Czech Republic and Slovakia.

Cities/Points of Interest:

Little can be said about the country of the Czech Republic. Communist rule, separation from Slovakia and a constant push to become part of modern Europe are always in the midst. Like many, I did not venture far outside of Prague for many reasons. The Czechs use the Cyrillic alphabet that is indecipherable unless one has taken courses in the language. Few outside of Prague speak English and it could be very difficult to travel and get around with the language barrier so evident. Unless you are the extremely adventurous type or have some background in the Czech language I advise you to stay close to Prague. There is plenty in the city to keep one occupied for an extended period of time.

Prague

The only European city not to be bombed during either World War, Prague maintains some of the most remarkable and pristine buildings in Europe. After exiting the train station it took a hefty walk to get to the town's center.

Inside Prague's public square is a reaching astrological clock tower blackened by years of standing tall in the city's centre. It chimes on the hour and like many of the European clock towers has a cute display at high noon. In the same public

square is a bustling marketplace of merchants and artisans selling their merchandise to tourists and locals alike. This area is crowded and very loud with the conversations of dozens of different languages and the traditional Czech bands playing for tips.

The public square has everything from blacksmiths molding iron to form traditional Czech souvenirs to a petting zoo for the kids. It is a great place to mingle with other cultures and see what Prague has to offer.

Prague is also known for its Jewish quarter. Many Jews lived here prior to WWII and to this day make up a large population of Prague's demographics. No matter where you walk in the Jewish quarter there is a synagogue, Jewish cemetery or other landmark on every block. The influence of the Jewish population has definitely played an effect on the way Prague is today.

After exiting the pedestrian areas lined with shops, the next logical step is to cross Charles IV Bridge to the Castle District. The famous bridge is lined with

Charles IV Bridge spanning the Vlatava River

statues and has become a Mecca for Prague artists to sell and inspire their work. Painters, musicians, and jewelry makers are spaced out within steps of each other and are the cause for stopped traffic as tourists pause to look at each of the artisan's works.

Just on the other side of the bridge is a near vertical hike up a hill to the Castle District. As expected the hill is lined with shop and restaurants. It sits on top of the city and has dozens of castles and estates belonging to the royal government. Some of the cathedrals and palaces can be seen on a tour, but this is the most tourist filled spot in Prague. There are hundreds of kids, grandparents, families, and tour groups all hoping to see the same sites and get on tours. It can be a little overwhelming and slightly frustrating. I chose to walk about the complex looking at each of the buildings and if one was less crowded I walked in. After that I grabbed an ice cream from a nearby vendor and sat on the wall overlooking the entire city of Prague.

Europe has done a great job to provide tourists with some of the best views imaginable. Whether placing certain sites on a hill for defense or a bridge to connect old and new cities, Europe is never low on providing visitors with good views. At the top of the hill in the castle district is a view of the terra cotta colored rooftops, the Vltava River, Charles IV bridge, vineyards and a smaller, distant replica of the Eiffel Tower. Gustav Eiffel, the architect behind the famous Parisian monument, built another monument in the hills surround Prague. So if you look far enough in the distance from your spot on top of the wall you might be able to see the Eiffel Tower!

National Holidays	
January 1	New Year's Day and Day of Restoration of Independent Czech State
March/April	Easter Monday
May 1	May Day
May 8	Liberation Day
July 5	SS Cyril and Methodius'Day
July 6	Jan Hus Day
September 28	Czech Statehood Day
October 28	Independence Day
November 17	Day of Fight for Freedom and Democracy
December 24	Christmas Eve
December 25	Christmas Day
December 26	St. Stephen's Day

Denmark

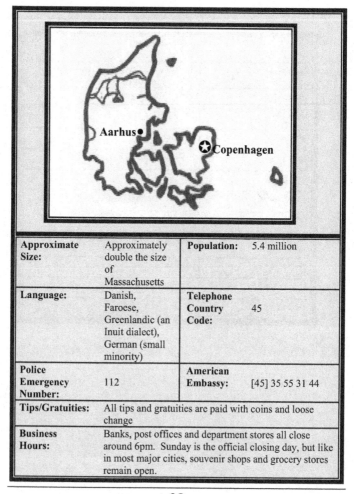

Approximate Size:	Approximately double the size of Massachusetts	Population:	5.4 million
Language:	Danish, Faroese, Greenlandic (an Inuit dialect), German (small minority)	Telephone Country Code:	45
Police Emergency Number:	112	American Embassy:	[45] 35 55 31 44
Tips/Gratuities:	All tips and gratuities are paid with coins and loose change		
Business Hours:	Banks, post offices and department stores all close around 6pm. Sunday is the official closing day, but like in most major cities, souvenir shops and grocery stores remain open.		

History and Overview:

The Golden Age for Denmark included the time during the Viking Period from the 9th-11th centuries. It was through these people that Christianity was brought to Denmark and foreign goods and conquests helped to boost the economy. The small mainland is supported by over four hundred islands, forming obstacles between the North and Baltic Seas. This forced much of the maritime activity to go through the hands of the Danes and to further increase power over the waters of Northern Europe.

Queen Margaret is credited for uniting Denmark, Finland, Sweden, Norway, the Faroe Islands, Greenland and Iceland. This is a primary reason why many of the Scandinavian countries today contain the same traditions, architecture, and philosophies. It was when the Reformation hit Denmark in the early 16th century that the people converted to Protestantism. To this day over 85% of the Danish population is Lutheran.

Cities/Points of Interest:

Nothing gives a more surreal feeling of being in Scandinavia than traveling throughout Denmark. It is a small country and not one widely visited by tourists, which only adds to its charm. Reaching it can be difficult if you are coming from a location farther away. There are no Ryan Air terminals located in Denmark and only one international airport. Unless you fly into Copenhagen, the only option other than by boat is to take the train leading from Germany.

The main tourist destination in Denmark is Copenhagen. It is the capital and provides the most accommodations and sites for a visitor. Other quick places of interest are Legoland, numerous islands, the cities of Odense and Århus, and Hamlet's castle in Shakespeare's famous play. Kronborg (the name of Hamlet's castle) is just north of Copenhagen, but amusement parks and more rural points of interest are on the mainland. Much of Denmark consists of islands connected by bridges and tunnels both for cars and trains. Copenhagen is also located on one of the most eastern islands.

Copenhagen

Just a quick train trip from the Swedish border, Copenhagen gives the crisp and clean feeling of a Scandinavian town. The multi-colored houses are all lined along the canals with flat fronts and many windows pointing to the water. The main mode of transportation in this town is by bike, which at some points can be quite brave considering the cold temperatures. Due to the nature of islands making up Denmark, Copenhagen consists of many canals and bridges linking the city together to provide for an interconnecting series of streets, and parts of town.

The Royal Palace is a sprawling complex with much more grounds than can originally be seen. You can walk into the courtyard and look at how the Royals

live or take the guided tour. My favorite part of the city is the huge park in the middle of Copenhagen. Trees line each side of the grassy plain as even more houses point inward toward the view of the park. A tree lined walkway leads from one side of the park to the other giving yet another view of marvelous buildings and the Royal Palace.

Copenhagen is a relatively quiet, understated town without the bells and whistles of other major European capitals. It is a relaxing and a representative look at the Scandinavian way of life and a more home-like city than others.

National Holidays	
January 1	New Year's Day
March/April	Maundy Thursday
March/April	Good Friday
March/April	Easter Monday
April/May	Great Prayer Day
May/June	Ascension Day
May/June	Pentecost Monday
June 5	Constitution Day
December 24	Christmas Eve
December 25	Christmas Day
December 26	St. Stephen's Day
December 31	New Year's Eve

England

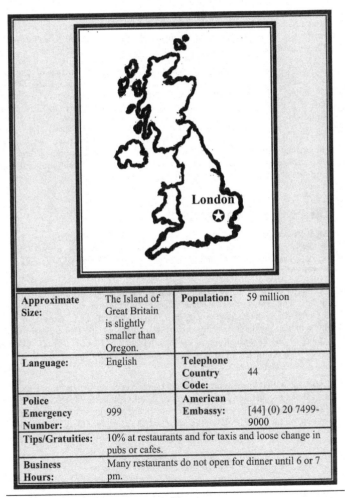

London ✪

Approximate Size:	The Island of Great Britain is slightly smaller than Oregon.	Population:	59 million
Language:	English	Telephone Country Code:	44
Police Emergency Number:	999	American Embassy:	[44] (0) 20 7499-9000
Tips/Gratuities:	10% at restaurants and for taxis and loose change in pubs or cafes.		
Business Hours:	Many restaurants do not open for dinner until 6 or 7 pm.		

History and Overview:

England has played an instrumental role in European history since the prehistoric ages. It was in this time that stone settlements rose up; the most important one to note is the famous Stonehenge. Under Roman Emperor Julius Caesar, Rome expanded to Britain and eventually to the border zone between England and Scotland. At this narrowest part of the island, Roman Emperor Hadrian built a huge wall fortification to keep the Barbarians to the north contained and his Roman citizens and British counterparts protected.

The English have dealt with a lot of invasions over its long history. The Romans, Saxons, Angles, Vikings, Scots, French, and others have tested their might against the English. In its history, England also saw Absolutism, The Plague, civil war, a revolution, and a great fire.

Not to be deterred by years of hardship, the English were the first to take away absolutist rule from their king with the signing of the Magna Carta in 1215. There were also movements for the codification of laws and individual rights. The rise of the Tutors, most importantly Elizabeth I, gave way to Shakespeare, strong government, and rights for the people.

The British Empire expanded after uniting with the Scottish crown, overthrowing the Spanish Armada, and colonizing in North America. Centuries of invasions, wars, advances, and setbacks, have kept the English very multi-cultural and a leading nation among the world.

Cities/Points of Interest:

Most American tourists look forward to traveling to England and London primarily because English is spoken and there is no trouble with a language barrier. Do not be so sure though. Some English have such thick accents that it is still just as difficult to decipher what they are saying.

One thing to keep in mind about England and London in particular is to plan ahead. This city is too crowded, too big, and too expensive to just wing it. Probably the most expensive city in Europe, you will find yourself spending more money per day than anywhere else in Europe. To buy a meal from an American fast food chain it cost me the equivalent of 12 U.S. Dollars. Look for deals offered on signs outside of restaurants or be thrifty by buying some meals at a grocery store.

I will focus this chapter primarily on London because that is by far the most visited and popular destination for travelers to England. The English countryside does possess great alternatives to city travel and more local sites, but hesitations to drive on the opposite side of the road and the close proximity of national sites in London tends to draw the most visitors.

London

London in recent years has become one of the most culturally diverse cities in Europe. Once mocked for its bad food, London has begun incorporating different cultures and menus into its once sub-par culinary sector. Indian, Asian, and Caribbean style restaurants give visitors opportunities to stray away from the traditional English cuisine to other more adventurous types.

Did you know that London is actually the smallest city in the world? Technically London consists only of a one square mile piece of land, but once metropolitan areas are included, London quickly becomes a much larger city in the world ranking. For this reason it is smart to stop at a local tourist office or do research before leaving for London. There are countless sights and museums to see and it would be impossible to hit everything without having a plan.

By far the easiest way to get around London is by taking advantage of the subway system or what locals call, "The Tube." Stops and signs are organized in such a way that it is extremely easy to understand and navigate the large city without aimlessly walking on the busy streets. I advise for however long you're there to buy an unlimited Tube pass. You will use the tube to go down the street, to cross the town and to get to the airport. It is worth spending the money and worth avoiding the hassle of navigating the busy roads.

One thing to watch for is that the majority of the Tube lines stop running at 11 pm. This becomes difficult when going out to a pub at night or to a Soho club because you must leave early in order to catch the last train or pay the sometimes expensive cost of a taxi fare back to your hostel. In the tube stations you will regularly hear a man or woman over the loudspeaker telling you to "Mind the Gap." This is the English way to notify the tourists to watch out for the gap between the platform and the train itself. On one occasion the man over the loudspeaker said, "Lady in the green sweater, please extinguish your smoke." I guess they are always watching you.

One concern and annoyance while traveling in England is the rainy weather and sometimes grey days. It is true that it rains practically everyday, but it's unnecessary to always use the umbrella. The rains are usually quick and light. There were times I would go into the tube stop when it was raining and come back up five minutes later and it was sunny. You will get tired of putting your umbrella up and down every time a rain comes; just use your hood and wait it out for a few minutes before opting to put up the hand-occupying nuisance.

Sundays are difficult days to sightsee in London. Museums are only open for a couple hours during the day and most tourists find this to be the premium time to visit them. Stay away from tourist sites on Sundays; instead walk through any of the free and sprawling sights of London. It can be just as enjoyable to walk through the Kew Gardens, Hyde Park, or the flea markets set up on Sundays.

If not planned, you could spend most of your time in London walking all across the city to one of the hundreds of places of interest. London has a lot of green space ideal to take walks or to take a break with a picnic. St. James Park, the

Mall with Buckingham Palace, and Notting Hill could each take an entire day to appreciate.

Take a moment to note the proximity of the sites from one another. From Big Ben and the Parliament building it is a rather short walk to pass No. 10 Downing Street, the residence of the Prime Minister, and then onto Trafalgar Square. Trafalgar Square is filled with hurried pedestrians and dozens of red double decker busses. A statue to commemorate Horatio Nelson, who defeated the

Spanish Armada at the Battle of Trafalgar, stands in the middle of the square shops, restaurants, and simply just to watch the diverse people passing by every moment.

From Trafalgar Square the road leads right to the Mall eventually passing St. James

St. James Park

Park and ending at Buckingham Palace. The Royal Residence is packed with tourists and it is nearly impossible to get a spot near the gate. The always popular changing of the guard occurs at noon everyday, but if you want to get a view you need to get a spot well in advance. Tours of the building are only allowed in the months of August and September and even then it is difficult to get a place on the tour. Walking on to the left, backside of the Palace is where you can get your chance to take a photo with one of the emotionless Royal Guardsmen. Not much farther away is another London popular site: one of those many red telephone booths. Yes, my friends and I tried to see how many we could fit inside—for the record it's five.

London has some of the best museums in the world and I was lucky enough to visit most of them. Take the time to visit the National Gallery, the Tate Museum, London Museum, Albert and Victoria, and others that call London home. You can view the sarcophagus of King Tut, The Rosetta Stone, paintings from the world's most famous artists and documents that changed the history of the world. Here as well as most other museums, headsets can be purchased to give an audio self-guided tour of the museums.

When visiting London do not miss the opportunity to see one of its plays. London's theatre district in Soho is equivalent to Broadway in New York City. You can purchase day-of tickets or tickets days in advance to see some of the most acclaimed and popular plays. There are ticket offices near the theatres that offer discounted prices. These prices change daily and differ from office to office, but are clearly displayed so that you can compare prices and pick the show you most want to see. I purchased tickets to see Les Meserables the day before the show for only 20 U.S. Dollars. The theatres are small and laid out with stadium seating so that even the worst seat is a good seat. Dress is relatively casual and the performances are beyond comparison. Leaving London without seeing a play is like going to Italy and not eating pasta.

Other famous landmarks that London is known for are: the Tower of London, The London Eye, Madam Toussaud's Wax Museum, St. Paul's Cathedral, and

Westminster Abbey

Westminster Abbey. Each of these sites, though famous and worth visiting, is very expensive. The Tower of London was the largest fortress in Medieval Europe and now acts as a museum to show cells, dungeons, torture devices, and other highlights. It costs around 40 U.S. Dollars to take the tour. I personally was not willing to spend the money and visit, but those who opted to later told me they wish they hadn't spent the money. However, if you have budgeted money properly and want to see the Tower of London then treat yourself to a tour.

The London Eye is a giant ferris wheel on the banks of the Thames that gives a panoramic view of the entire city from each of its compartments. It takes about 45 minutes for the Eye to make a full rotation and costs nearly a dollar a minute. The view is great, but another thing I felt to be overpriced.

Madam Toussaud's wax museum is a fun diversion from normal, historical and influential sites. There are wax figures of celebrities and historical people done to the smallest detail making them exactly the same dimensions as the actual personality. The great thing is that unlike most museums you are allowed to touch. You can stand next to Steven Spielberg and realize just how short he is in real life or stand next to President Lincoln and see how gangly he was. You can also have your picture taken with your arm around Brad Pitt. There are few discounts and the prices of the tickets vary due to the time of day. This is an expensive attraction, but it can occupy a couple of hours as you stroll through the celebrities.

Westminster Abbey is known by many and for that reason it tends to be one of the more crowded places in London. Get here early because the line soon wraps around the building and continues down the street. There are two separate entrances and lines that eventually funnel visitors into the Abbey. Don't be surprised to wait at least an hour and a half to get in. Like all other place in London, Westminster has an entrance fee and is crowded with tourists. Give yourself a window of at least three hours to see this site because of the line and the crowded struggle to see the inside. Along with the altar and pews for service much of the Abbey acts as a tomb for thousands of London's finest. You can see the tomb of Sir Isaac Newton as well as many members of the English Royal Family. I felt Westminster to be creepy and morbid. It is a must-see due to the structure itself and the importance that it embodies, but the crowds are less than appealing.

There are low-cost alternatives to seeing London though. Pubs offer cheaper drinks and an opportunity to meet the locals. Bars in Soho are very expensive and usually require the equivalent to a $20 cover. Visiting a pub gives a more local experience and a cheaper English lager.

Another cheap alternative is to watch a session of British Parliament. It is free to attend and you can comfortably watch as the Lords barrage each other with insults and degradations. The line (or queue as the English call it) begins early and does not guarantee you a seat, but the couple hours to watch a session is very entertaining and free!

I mentioned earlier that London has an immense amount of green space. Take a walk through the gardens and parks to soak in the atmosphere of the city. Inside Hyde Park is Kensington Palace. Everyday they offer tea where you can participate in the English ritual and see a landmark at the same time.

Finally, the best and most advised activity is to take a cruise on the Thames. Ticket fare is relatively inexpensive and the open-air ferry takes guest on a cruise down the River Thames with a commentary from a witty and sometimes cynical guide. You will start by the London Eye and continue down past St. Paul's Cathedral, the Tower of London, Tower Bridge (also known by Americans as London Bridge) and the Globe Theatre before arriving later into the town of Greenwich.

Greenwich is most known as the location of the Prime Meridian and the separation of the Eastern and Western Hemispheres. There is a huge park with trees and flowers leading from the National Maritime Museum and the entrance of the complex to the observatory at the top of the hill. The observatory has clocks and telescopes, but most importantly it has the world clock and the line designating the prime meridian.   This quaint town with vintage shops, reconstructed ships, museums, and a park is a great afternoon excursion from the high-paced city of London.

National Holidays	
January 1	New Year's Day
March/April	Good Friday
March/April	Easter Monday
1st Monday in May	May Day
Last Monday in May	Spring Bank Holiday
Last Monday in August	Summer Bank Holiday
December 25	Christmas Day
December 26	Boxing Day

France

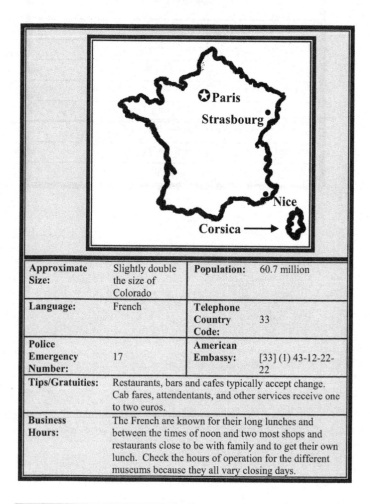

Approximate Size:	Slightly double the size of Colorado	Population:	60.7 million
Language:	French	Telephone Country Code:	33
Police Emergency Number:	17	American Embassy:	[33] (1) 43-12-22-22
Tips/Gratuities:	Restaurants, bars and cafes typically accept change. Cab fares, attendants, and other services receive one to two euros.		
Business Hours:	The French are known for their long lunches and between the times of noon and two most shops and restaurants close to be with family and to get their own lunch. Check the hours of operation for the different museums because they all vary closing days.		

History and Overview:

The most influential period in France was throughout the 18th Century during the time of the Louis. This is the time that has molded France into the country it is today and a defining reason why the French have turned quite "cold" in some areas.

France was dominated by absolute monarchies, the most famous being that of Louis XIV. He built the grandiose Palace at Versailles and spent obscene amounts of money on military campaigns, extravagant art and architecture. Some of the most popular French painters like Jacques-Louis David were patrons to Louis. All of the money the King spent to hire architects, painters, and personal assistants led to financial problems for France and eventually to discontent and the French Revolution.

After the tumultuous time of the Revolution and the Guillotine, Napoleon soon took power and expanded his empire to the borders of Russia. The French people began to distrust government officials and the government in general. Also, century-long feuds with England and rather current border disputes with Germany during the World Wars have caused France to stay more to itself these days and focus on their own country.

Cities/Points of Interest:

Europe's largest country and home to famous tourist destinations like Paris, Normandy and the French Riviera; France has remained one of the most visited countries in Europe. Americans typically have a stereotype of the French, and I feel an unjust one. In all of my experiences in France whether traveling alone or in small groups, the locals were always more than willing to help me. It is true that if you automatically begin speaking in English to them, they will pretend to not understand or completely ignore the inquiry. Make an effort to approach them with asking, "Do you speak English" in French. "Parlez vous Anglais?" The French are very helpful and eager to assist as long as you give them respect by not automatically assuming they speak English.

France has a phenomenal transportation system and probably the best subway structure on the continent. Most of the train lines run through Paris and it is typical to take high-speed trains lines (the TGV) through the nation's capital in order to go elsewhere. Take advantage of the Metro (this is what the French call their subway) by purchasing a carnat (pronounced car-nay) of tickets. You can buy a 10 pack or 20 pack for the equivalent of 1€ a ticket. Like in all other transportation services be sure to validate the ticket because in some instances conductors will check that riders have valid tickets. Simply slide the carnat into the machine, automatic doors will open and you are free to take the Metro to your next location. This system even enables you to switch lines without being forced to use another ticket. Be prepared to see it all while on the Metro. On one trip alone there was an aspiring Karaoke singer gracing me with her talents and a couple sitting directly in front of me engaging in R-rated extra-curricular activities. Use your imagination....

While in France make an effort to try one of the many culinary dishes the French are known for. French onion soup, crêpes, fondue and many of the regional specialties are some of the best dishes you will try while in Europe. Often times a glass of wine is cheaper than the bottled water; so if you are in the mood to try local specialties go for the deep red of the Bordeaux wines while in the region. Here is a quick lesson in French dining. If you ask for the *menu*, you will receive a predetermined meal of the day. If you ask for *la carte* the waiter will bring you what we consider a menu listing the dishes offered.

An entire vacation could be spent in France alone, so it is necessary to decide what you most want to see. In the North are towns with great cathedrals and the historical importance of Normandy and the D-Day invasion. In the South is the luxury and wealth of the French Riviera giving way to afternoons by the Mediterranean. In other areas one can wander the vineyards of Provence and Bordeaux, the chateâus in the Loire Valley, or the ever famous stop of Paris. The decision is yours, and France is never short on providing visitors with some of the best sites in Europe.

Paris

Paris is nothing short of every expectation I had for it. Although somewhat cliché, Paris is easily my favorite city in Europe. The history and influence it has played on the world can be seen on nearly every corner and through its innumerable sites. Everyone is familiar with the Eiffel Tower and Notre Dame, but there is much more depth and many more surprises Paris has to offer that it could easily take a week to see and do everything.

Since Paris is in such high demand it is necessary to make reservations for accommodations. Prices for hotels and hostels are more expensive here than most places. I was fortunate to find a great hostel for 25€ a night only blocks away from the Louvre and a Metro stop. Although this is second only to the fare at my London hostel the location and atmosphere of staying in Paris was worth it.

Many of the sites are flooded with tourists, so at times fighting the crowd can be exhausting. Be sure to arrive at many of the most popular places early because the lines are much shorter. The Eiffel Tower is clearly the landmark of Paris. Huge lines form from each one of the four feet of the tower. There are three

Eiffel Tower at night

levels in the tower and prices vary on which level you wish to see. The top level is clearly the most expensive, but the view more than makes up for the wait in line and price. Building codes require that all buildings (with few exceptions) stay at four stories or less providing for an indescribable view over the city of Paris. At the summit, other Paris landmarks are clearly visible and noted. You can look down and see the Champs- Elyssé, l'hôtel des Invalides or pont neuf.

The Arc de Triomphe immediately draws your attention because the arch constructed by Napoleon in the early nineteenth century is now encircled by a chaotic ring and side streets with hundreds of cars changing lanes, honking horns, and narrowly missing other vehicles. The étoile as locals call it, or star, is a site that should not be missed. It is magnificent to see the arch at the center of modern day innovation.

Leading from the Arc de Triomphe is the grand boulevard of the Champs-Elyssé. The most famous street in Paris is home to some of the most high-end retailers like Louis Vuitton (the building looks like a giant Vuitton bag) and Cartier. Walking the 2-mile long boulevard is a great way to see the high life of sophisticated Paris. At the end of the Champs-Elyssé is a large obelisk and closely behind it is the Louvre.

The Louvre is the most famous museum in Paris and the most famous museum in Europe. This museum houses sculptures from artists like Venus de Milo and paintings by all the great artists like Vermeer and Da Vinci. The *Mona Lisa* is tucked back in the west wing of the Louvre. Guests are required to keep a continual walking flow past it and absolutely no photos are allowed. The camera flash is damaging to paintings. Even if you are not an art lover this museum is essential. If you only go to one museum on your trip the Louvre should be it. One money saving tip is that on the first Sunday of every month all of the museums in Paris including the Louvre, Museé D'Orsay, and others are free. Arrive early to beat the crowd and see all of the famous artists and paintings you have only read about in books.

Other famous sites not to be missed are: l'Hotel des Invalides, which chronicles the history of the French military and is home to Napoleon's tomb, The Notre Dame Cathedral and le Sacré Coeur located on top of Montmartre on the Western side of the city. The interesting architecture, white façade and expansive

Sacré Coeur

interior of the Sacré Coeur can only be surpassed by its view of the city. You can sit atop a rock wall at the foot of the church's steps and look over the city and see Notre Dame, the River Seine and the Eiffel Tower in the background. This area of Paris is less crowded and provides for a quick time away from large tour groups and to have a moment to experience Paris quietly.

A short walk down the hill and onto a main road soon puts you into the Red Light District of Paris and eventually to the famed Moulin Rouge. This area is quite dirty, littered with porn shops and prostitution and is easily forgettable. The red windmill seen in the movie is a long walk from the starting point and a veritable disappointment. Avoid this area known for crime and drugs and attend other areas more fun for college-aged tourists.

The Latin Quarter on the right bank of the River Seine is a great place to find hostels and nighttime activities. This area was once called the Latin Quarter because it housed universities that were only taught in Latin and has now become an area filled with students, artists, and the young-at-heart. The Latin Quarter is close to Metro stops, landmarks, and some inexpensive hostels for tourists.

Paris has constructed a fabulous and organized Metro system, but sometimes the best way to get around is to walk the city streets. Along the banks of the River Seine are sidewalks that bikers, couples or individuals reading books take advantage of to get a more intimate feeling with Paris. River cruises are plentiful but many times overcrowded and over-priced.

The Tuliers Gardens and les Jardins du Luxembourg are sprawling areas of green space in the middle of the city to relax and have a chat with a local. If you would like to take a break at a café it should not be difficult considering there is one within a stones throw of wherever you are. My roommate, however, took me on a hunt for the only Starbucks in Paris. During our search we luckily stumbled upon the Opera House which is right down the promenade. The building in itself is unbelievable, but the inside is much more awe-inspiring.

Paris really does live up to all the expectations and stories you may have heard. The opportunity to stand atop the Eiffel Tower is a feeling you will never forget. After the loudness and craziness of the city it may by preferable to take excursions to the countryside or lesser visited towns.

Strasbourg

This French city lying on the German border is a great day trip to experience a different type of French culture. During the World Wars there were land disputes between France and Germany over the provinces of Alsace and Lorraine which contain the city of Strasbourg. The French eventually

gained control of the territory but there is still a heavy emphasis on German culture.

Half-timbered buildings and coo-coo clocks are in abundance as well as the traditional French music played by street performers. It is not unusual to hear both French and German being spoken, considering the German border can be seen just past the Danube River.

Strasbourg is a great place to go shopping, but this town is best seen by one of the many boat tours offered. The two-hour long tours wind through the city in completely glassed in boats with audio headsets in the language of your choice. You can visit the area known as *le Petite France* and see one of the many international buildings centered in Strasbourg. And lastly, in the center of town is the Notre Dame Cathedral that is a close replica to the more popular version in Paris.

Strasbourg is a small city without the grandiose monuments and historical significance as other places in France, but it is a good day trip to see the blending of French and German culture along with the less visited, more relaxed setting.

Nice

In the South, hugging the Mediterranean is the city of Nice (pronounced like niece). This port city generally acts as a home base to visitors. Monaco is only a thirty-minute train ride away and leaves regularly. To the west of Nice are the cities of the French Riviera: Caans, St. Tropez, St. Moritz, etc. Taking a train

ride along the coast gives great views and hundreds of photo opportunities.

After leaving the train station, walk le promenade leading to the beach. This long street is lined with shops and cafes and enables the time to soak in the rays of Southern France. At the end of le promenade are city parks and the entrance into le vieille ville, or old city. This part of Nice is adjacent to the beach and has cobble-stoned streets, older buildings and flower markets in the open squares. The aroma from the flowers fill the old city and give a nostalgic feeling of what life must have been like.

Don't be surprised once you come upon the beach, because instead of sand there are rather decent sized rocks. There are over a dozen private beaches and included for a fee are chairs, umbrellas, and other great services to accommodate your time sitting along the Mediterranean soaking in the weather. Be prepared to find many of the beaches to be topless. This is generally the norm rather than just a few daring souls letting their exhibitionism show.

And finally there is the Ferry Port in Nice. It is the debarkation point for many ferries going to Marseilles, Sardinia, and Corsica. Ferries are rather expensive, but the view of the Mediterranean and a side trip to one of the nearby islands is a good excursion. Whether Nice is your home base or primary destination, the city's great weather, clean streets and abundance of excursion options make it a premium choice city to visit.

Corsica

After a six-hour ferry ride from Nice, you can end up on the striking island of Corsica. Its fine sand beaches and mountainous interior make Corsica a diverse and intriguing island to discover. Most of the ferries dock in either Bastia or Ajaccio. I spent the majority of my stay in Ajaccio because it was farther south and catered more to tourists. Ajaccio has a large harbor with hundreds of boats waiting for the chance to set sail on the open waters. It is also the birthplace of Napoleon and countless monuments, souvenirs, and businesses are named after the former Emperor.

Hostels are few, if not non-existent in Corsica because few college-aged backpackers make this a stop on their agenda. Hotels are typically expensive

and may attempt to trick you into paying more for the room than you originally agreed upon. As a standard rule, make it a point to discuss the rate of the room before checking in. This prevents trickery and inflated hotel prices.

English is also not spoken prevalently. You will find those who do speak English, but due to

Ajaccio harbor

the fewer amounts of tourists and the thriving Movement for Independence, it is not as easy to find English speakers in Corsica as it would be in Paris or Nice.

Buses leave sporadically for other areas on the island and can offer alternatives to visit the interior rather than remaining stationary. The bus is usually headed by some old, eccentric driver that takes the hairpin turns around the mountainous

cliffs at a frightening 60 miles per hour. There is no direct route to the other cities because of the rolling mountains which turns the 50-mile trip into nearly two and a half hours of a terrifying bus ride.

Corte, Corsica

There is not much to do on Corsica other than to enjoy the beaches and the weather of the incredible island located in the Mediterranean Sea.

National Holidays	
January 1	New Year's Day
March/April	Easter Monday
May 1	May Day
May 8	VE Day
May	Ascension Day
May/June	Pentecost Monday
August 15	Assumption of the Virgin
November 1	All Saints' Day
November 11	Armistice Day
December 25	Christmas Day

Germany

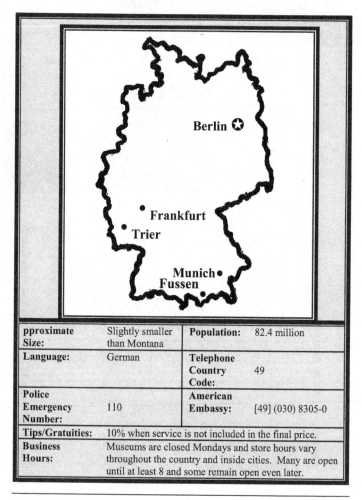

pproximate Size:	Slightly smaller than Montana	**Population:**	82.4 million
Language:	German	**Telephone Country Code:**	49
Police Emergency Number:	110	**American Embassy:**	[49] (030) 8305-0
Tips/Gratuities:	10% when service is not included in the final price.		
Business Hours:	Museums are closed Mondays and store hours vary throughout the country and inside cities. Many are open until at least 8 and some remain open even later.		

History and Overview:

Surprisingly, Germany is a relatively young country by European standards. It wasn't until 1871 when Otto Von Bismarck finally unified all of the German provinces that make up present day Germany. Prior to unification Germany was split into hundreds of different political and tribal groups. Although the people were united, the division in regional cultures and dialects is still great.

Germany has always been a military state whether as a unified country or during its times as fragmented tribes. Emperor Wilhelm I expanded military power, thus causing tension and leading to World War I. After the loss in the First World War, Hitler gained power through the Socialist party and eventually sparked the Second World War. The loss of this War in 1945 split the country into East and West. East Germany was communist while West Germany was a Republic and aligned with the U.S., U.K. and France. The city of Berlin was also divided into East and West with a wall constructed between the two. The East Germans were isolated from non-communist Europe while their western counterparts enjoyed the freedoms that democracy brings. In early 1989 the Berlin wall was torn down, Germany was again unified, and the separation between East and West was officially abandoned. People could once again travel freely throughout Germany.

The Germans are a great military power and extremely efficient in industry. This prowess is not only limited to tanks and machinery, but to transportation and road works. Traveling around Germany may be the easiest and best run in Europe today.

Cities/Points of Interest:

The country that surprised me the most with its people and abundance of sites was Germany. Each region of the country provides the traveler with different customs and a completely different atmosphere. You can visit the enormity of Berlin or the small villages of places like Fussen. The Germans tend to get a bad wrap due to stereotypes and preconceived notions of those still feeling they belong to the once Fascist Nazi Germany; this is entirely not the case. I struck up more conversations and met more locals interested in chatting than anywhere else in Europe. Check all stereotypes at the door. Give each country a chance to prove their generosity and show what they have to offer.

Berlin

Berlin is the largest city in Germany and eight times the size of Paris. It resides on the far Eastern side of the country. It is difficult to grasp how large Berlin is, but it's important to accommodate this factor because there is much to see in the capital city, and often it takes much more time to negotiate than originally expected.

Give yourself ample time to peruse the streets of Berlin. The recent history of the world wars and other tourist sites are worth seeing while in the city. You will definitely use the public transportation here more than almost any other

place in Europe due to the size and sprawl of the city. The Germans have mastered public transportation and I find it overall to be the best in Europe and possibly in the world. There is the U-bahn, which is a subway, the S-Bahn that is an elevated train,

The Reichstag, Berlin

trams dominating the streets, and endless taxis and public buses are available. Berlin is the place to purchase a weekend unlimited pass or a group of tickets at one time. This eliminates the hassle of constantly buying tickets and in the end saves you money.

World War II ended only 60 years ago, but the East/West dichotomy and separation is still very apparent. The famous Brandenburg Gates which stood as a symbol dividing the city, now is open as tourists and locals alike stroll in and out of the only city gate in Berlin. In the East, graffiti still dominates the walls and construction zones are everywhere. The city is desperately trying to repair the old German quarter and make it equally as commercial and modern as the Western side of town.

The most surreal and poignant spots to see in Berlin are the old sections of the Berlin Wall still standing. The wall that was erected virtually overnight marked the separation between the East and West and in an unfortunate amount of cases, separated families and friends who lived on either side of the wall. Visit this divider and see the desperation and hope scrawled in graffiti all over the wall.

A portion of the Berlin Wall near Checkpoint Charlie

During the War Berlin was set up into four quarters: The British, American, Russian and German sectors. Checkpoint Charlie is one of the stations marking the border into the American sector. Today the booth stands and a nearby museum gives visitors a glimpse at life during the delineation between the sides and the many escape attempts made during the nineteen years the wall stood.

Berlin is home to some of the greatest museums in Europe, in particular, the Pergamonmuseum that has many ancient artifacts from digs around the world. There is the old museum and the new museum as well as the National Art Gallery. If you are interested in art or visiting these museums there is a day pass that gets visitors into every museum with the purchase of only one ticket.

To see more grandiose art and architecture take a quick break from the city and venture to Potsdam on the outskirts of Berlin. The old palace built for Kaiser Wilhelm II was also home to conferences during the Wars.

Finally, to enjoy a relaxing meal or some shopping while in Berlin visit the Alexanderplatz. It is an enormous marketplace with the occasional flea market and street vendors covering the open expanses of the square. The recognizable TV tower is located in the center of the square and the Berliner Dom, or Berlin Cathedral, is a nearby walk. This is a great place to take some time out from site seeing to relax, enjoy some wiener schnitzel and a nice German beer.

Munich and Bavaria

For the opportunity to break away from large cities and quick paced touring, take a relaxing stop in Munich. The city can be covered in a full day or spread over a couple, more relaxed days. Although one of Germany's biggest cities, Munich has managed to keep its small town appeal. The Bavarian culture and liveliness is prevalent from the pedestrian-only center, to the beer halls that make Munich famous.

The information office at the train station is one of the most helpful and accommodating tourist offices I found. The staff is willing to provide maps and suggestions of activities, hostels, and good places to eat.

Leading from the main train station to the Residenz, or palace, is the pedestrian walk that is the must-do of Munich. Kaufingerstrasse and

The Glockenspiel

Neuhauserstrasse are the way to see the most popular sites of the city without having to carry a travel book. These streets pass by specialty shops, musky, candlelit restaurants, past the glockenspiel (mechanical carillon) to street performers, the Bavarian Parliament Building, to the palace, and then to the world famous Haufbrauhaus.

The Haufbrauhaus is a great way to experience a "traditional" German beer hall. Now much of the building is open to an abundance of travelers, but for the price and the atmosphere this is quickly forgotten and you almost feel as if you are a part of the German way of life. The hall is extremely crowded with few open seats. Look carefully to find a place to sit, but be cautious to not sit in one of the regulars' seats. This will not go over well with the locals or the waitresses use to serving them.

Munich can be very expensive and crowded at times along the Marionplatz, the heavily trafficked pedestrian area. There is a lot to do along the route but there is much more outside the city to experience.

A quick train ride to the outskirts of the city is the remnants of the old concentration camp at Daachu. This historical site and emotional trial is quite accessible and has a museum and a guided English tour included in the price of admission. If this is your only chance to experience the tragedy of the holocaust, Daachu is an easy and good site to visit. However, the museum is less raw and more museum-like than other camps like Auschwitz.

Another quick train ride from Munich is the small village of Fussen merely an hour away. This quiet town nestled between the German and Austrian border is

a purely peaceful and picturesque town, only imagined in fairy tales. Maybe that is why it fittingly is home to Neuschwanstein, the castle sitting atop the hill that was used by Disney as the inspiration for *Sleeping Beauty's* castle. I did not find it necessary to take the tour inside, the best view and least expensive is from the town or the fields below looking up to the enormous castle.

Fussen, Germany

Fussen is a great town, quiet and less over-run with tourists. This was a great way to get out of the city and to experience a town in its purity. I absolutely adored Fussen.

Other German Cities

It would be impossible for me to list all that Germany has to offer in just a few short pages. Berlin and Munich are clearly the most visited cities in Germany, but there are many more that have their own attractions to offer. Hamburg is a big city illuminated at night with lights dotting the harbor and lights coming from the many buildings making up the area.

The Rhine

Frankfurt is known as "Little America" because it is home to one of the largest U.S. Military bases outside of the United States. It is possible to speak English without worry anywhere in Frankfurt.

Heidelberg lies just south of Frankfurt and is a small college town nestled between the sweeping green hills and the Rhine River. This is a great place to rest for the day. Many in the city are younger, college-aged students and the pedestrian only section of the town has a lot of shops, outdoor cafes, and beer halls. The fortress overlooks the city and it gives Heidelberg a medieval feeling.

Along the Rhine River is Cologne. Famous for its towering cathedral I found there is little to do in this town, but it is peaceful and a good stop on the route to visit other sites in nearby German towns or Belgium. The Rhine is an absolutely ethereal river, and if there is an opportunity to take a ride through small German towns along the way this is a great starting off point.

Finally on the far western border near Luxembourg is the small town of Trier. This city played an important role during the time of the Holy Roman Empire and the Porta Negra still stands in the city center as a reminder of its Roman influences. Directly across the street is the birthplace of Karl Marx. Trier is also a pilgrimage to many seeking spiritual relics. Inside the cathedral is what is said to be the tunic Christ was wearing when he was crucified. Today it is inside a temperature-controlled, airtight case, but can be viewed for free by any who wish to visit.

It truly is difficult to pinpoint the one or two places to visit when in Germany, because each is unique and has a different style to offer. The country is large, but in each region is a town that cannot be missed; whether it is the half-timbered houses of Bavaria, the Black Forest to the South, the Rhine River and green hills of the West or the open fields and flowers to the North. Each part of Germany is unique and could become an entire vacation in itself.

National Holidays	
January 1	New Year's Day
January 6	Epiphany (Bavaria, Baden Württemberg and Saxony Only)
March/April	Good Friday
March/April	Easter Monday
May	Ascension Day
May 1	Labor Day
May/June	Pentecost Monday
August 15	Assumption of the Virgin (Bavaria and Saarland only)
October 3	Day of German Unity
November 1	All Saints' Day (Baden-Württemberg, Bavaria, North Rhine-Westphalia, Rhineland-Palatinate and Saarland only)
December 25	Christmas Day
December 26	St. Stephen's Day

Greece

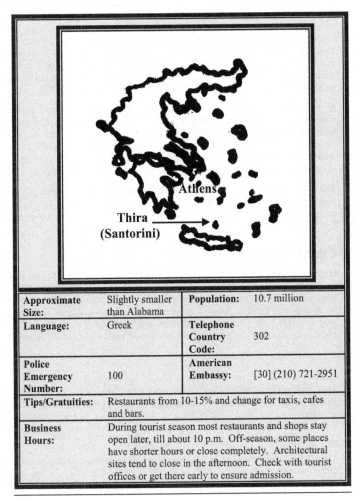

Approximate Size:	Slightly smaller than Alabama	**Population:**	10.7 million
Language:	Greek	**Telephone Country Code:**	302
Police Emergency Number:	100	**American Embassy:**	[30] (210) 721-2951
Tips/Gratuities:	Restaurants from 10-15% and change for taxis, cafes and bars.		
Business Hours:	During tourist season most restaurants and shops stay open later, till about 10 p.m. Off-season, some places have shorter hours or close completely. Architectural sites tend to close in the afternoon. Check with tourist offices or get there early to ensure admission.		

History and Overview:

The Greek society is one of the earliest in the world. Research and evidence date back early civilizations and fortifications to around 7000 b.c.e. (Before Common Era or b.c.). Greeks have always loved social interaction and entertainment. This zest for life is still incorporated into modern years by participating in siestas and taking everything more slowly and relaxed.

From the beginning, the Greeks had a very organized political and social system. In 776 b.c.e. the first Olympic Games were held. Greece was made up of fragmented city-states each with their own government; some were more militaristic like Sparta, while some were more democratic like Athens. The Greeks constantly felt as though they had to protect themselves from foreign invaders. Greece was one of the most highly developed civilizations in the world and an ideal conquest for other invaders. Many military campaigns occurred: the Trojan War in present-day Turkey, invasions by the Doric and Persian people, and inter-Greek fighting in the Peloponnesian War among other scuffles.

It is in Greece where the foundations for democracy were laid, coinage systems were founded, weights and measures established as well as a line of influential males in all fields. Aristotle, Socrates, and Plato advanced the fields of philosophy and government, Sophocles and Euripides furthered theatre, Homer wrote one of the most important books in history, Pythagoras gave us a basis in math, and Hippocrates is still cited today by every doctor around the world.

The rocky and island terrain, alongside its ancient history has morphed Greece into a modern European country with a distinctly ancient feel. The Greeks look to their prosperous times and use that as a basis to define themselves today.

Cities/Points of Interest:

Greece has one of the longest and most vibrant histories in the Mediterranean and Western World. During its dominance over the Mediterranean, the Greeks built and molded Athens into an astonishing city. Many vacations to Greece start in Athens and entail a ferry to some of the picturesque islands dotting the Aegean. This travel plan is what I stuck to, and I found after a couple of days of noise and pollution I was ready for the solitude and relaxed pace of the islands.

Athens

This ancient city contains some of the most magnificent and surreal historical sites of anywhere in the world. The smog, crowds, and often unattractive streets are clearly not the most positive parts of visiting Athens. Remember that the Greek capital had been around centuries before many present day countries were even formed.

Take Athens for what it is, dedicate only a couple of days, and then quickly escape to the mountains or the islands. It is likely that you will spend the majority of your time in the historical part of the city. This area includes the

Acropolis and Agora. On top of the hill known as the Acropolis, sits the Parthenon. It is unbelievable to touch one of the most famous and historical architectural sites in the world. Be sure to check hours of operation; it would be a shame to visit the Parthenon and not be able to explore the inside and view one of the two amphitheatres.

The Parthenon atop the Acropolis

View of Athens from the Acropolis

The Acropolis is easily the most visited area in Athens, so arrive early and have an idea of what you want to see to enable a rest stop in the hotel or at a restaurant during the extremely hot afternoons. Hiking even farther up the hill, viewers can gaze over the sprawling suburbs of Athens and take in the birds-eye view of the Agora, which sits directly below the hill.

We chose to take a dirt path leading from the top of the Acropolis down to the foot of the Agora. Few tourists follow this almost non-existent path, and opt instead for the paved and usually guided tours. This route gave my friends and me the chance to elude the crowds and stroll through the ruins of a civilization thriving around 500 b.c. all while hearing monks chanting in the background. The Agora means market place, and while the top of the hill stood for the religious and political centers, the agora was the area of every day life. It feels as though you are stepping back in time when you are picnicking beside the ruins of a once great empire.

Other notable places worth mentioning are the Natural Gardens known as Ethnikós Kípos and Monastiráki. Both are close to the historical city and should be visited.

Although the city is old and crime is prevalent, the 2004 Olympic Games in Athens made it much more accommodating and easier to get around. The subway system was revamped, roads were repaved, and buildings were touched up. Thanks to the Olympics, pedestrians no longer have to play chicken with oncoming cars, rarely yielding to the walkers. Stick to the metro and be particularly aware of where you want to go. Athens can be intimidating and slightly dangerous. Tour during the day, relax in the afternoon, shop and eat at night, but stick to crowded areas and remain alert of what is around you.

Excursions from Athens

Athens is a great place to visit with even better sites. Two days for me in the crowded city was more than enough. Greek history and the Greek landscape gives you alternatives to still experience Greece outside the major city.

The first suggestion of places to go is larger cities on the coast like Thessaloniki and Corfu. Usually these areas attract younger travelers and are not nearly as over-run as Athens.

For the history buff like me, smaller towns in the mountains and on the peninsula represent the Greek past with old monasteries and ancient ruins. Delphi, Marathon, Sparta and Tripoli have all played a vital role in Greek history and they have the historical sites less bombarded and lesser known than other areas.

Finally, the most popular and my suggestion for an excursion from Athens is to take a ferry or a cruise of the Greek Isles. The islands are exactly what you picture from the whitewashed buildings with blue roofs, to donkeys and beautiful white sand beaches. Each island is unique and has a distinctly different feel. Mykanos is a popular destination for travelers because it is only three hours from the Athenian port of Pireas to its resort areas. Hydra, Naxos, and Rhodes are other popular islands.

I chose to spend a longer time on the "high-speed" ferry (a whopping seven hours) to venture farther away to the island of Thira (more popularly known as Santorini). The active volcanic island is arched around a caldera where the tip of the volcano once rested. The island is quiet and quaint, but still has plenty of activities such as sun bathing on a black sand beach, riding a vespa around the island, or taking a cruise out in the bay to the caldera.

Thira (Santorini)

Santorini seemed to have an older demographic visiting there, so it was not the raging college experience I might have expected. It did, however, give me just what I wanted...relaxation and great weather. You cannot go wrong with any of the Greek Islands in the Aegean, and the week spent sailing through the thousands of islands is indescribable and a great way to wind down from an intense couple of days in Athens.

National Holidays	
January 1	New Year's Day
January 6	Epiphany
February/March	Shrove Monday
March 25	Independence Day
*April/May	Good Friday
*April/May	Easter Monday
May 1	Labor Day
May/June	Pentecost Monday
August 15	Assumption of the Virgin
October 28	Óchi Day
December 25	Christmas Day
December 26	St. Stephen's Day

*Greece observes the Orthodox calendar and dates may not correspond with Western calendar.

Hungary

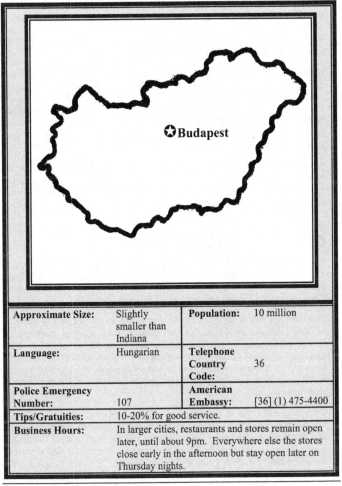

Approximate Size:	Slightly smaller than Indiana	Population:	10 million
Language:	Hungarian	Telephone Country Code:	36
Police Emergency Number:	107	American Embassy:	[36] (1) 475-4400
Tips/Gratuities:	10-20% for good service.		
Business Hours:	In larger cities, restaurants and stores remain open later, until about 9pm. Everywhere else the stores close early in the afternoon but stay open later on Thursday nights.		

History and Overview:

Although many Hungarians identify themselves with Western Europe, I believe it is their Eastern origins and influences that best define the country. Around the 5th century tribes migrated from areas of present-day Russia and settled in what is now Hungary. The tribes all lived in relative peace until the Mongols invaded during the 13th century. The devastation and terror wreaked upon the Hungarians stunted development for over one hundred years.

It was shortly after the Mongols that the Turks invaded. They reigned for over 150 years and split the country into three parts. The Hapsburgs controlled the East, Transylvanians controlled the South and the Turks controlled the rest. Out of defiance, many Hungarians took the Islamic symbol of the crescent moon, baked it into a fluffy bread and ate it to show their disgust with the Turkish rulers, hence the first croissant (and you probably thought it was French).

By the beginning of the 19th century the Hungarians retained power and then a national reform movement took hold. This was when the national anthem, academics and architectural brilliance took over. By 1873, Pest, Buda, and Obuda were unified making present-day Budapest a European metropolis. In this year the opera house, national gallery, and Parliament building were all constructed. Also, the first subsurface underground railway on continental Europe was put into operation.

Presently, seven different countries, each of which plays an influence on its culture surround Hungary. However, through years of gaining and losing territory, many ethnic Hungarians were displaced into neighboring countries and still to this day make up a large minority percentage.

Cities/Points of Interest:

The majority of tourists visiting Hungary go to see only one place, Budapest. This was the same in my case and I spent a few days in the old-feeling, Eastern European town. Although considered as Western Europe, the times of Communism and Eastern influence are vividly apparent in the city.

This could be one of the more challenging places to visit as an English-speaker because I found virtually no one that spoke English while in Budapest. The Hungarian language is not recognizable and nearly impossible to decipher a meaning. I suggest learning some key phrases or already have the name of your hotel and its address written down on a sheet of paper. This lessens confusion and the purely Hungarian speaking taxi driver can take you to your destination with no problem.

Petty theft and crime in Hungary seems oh-too common. Tourists on the train had passports and money stolen right out of their cabins while they were asleep, and the barrage of beggars when stepping off the train created diversions to allow thieves to go directly for your pockets. These first few moments in Budapest can be overwhelming and uncomfortable. That is why it is necessary to always have your money, passport, identification, and other valuable items on you at all times, preferably in a hidden money belt or pouch under your clothing. Pickpockets have no trouble taking something out of your pocket without you noticing but are unable to get to your belongings when they are in a moneybag inside your shirt or tucked under the belt of your pants. These safety precautions may seem annoying or unnecessary, but I assure you, this will save you the fear and hassle of having your personal effects stolen. A vacation can be totally ruined when you spend it at the American Embassy trying to get a new passport or on the phone trying to cancel credit cards.

Budapest

The capital of Hungary is actually divided into two parts, Buda and Pest. Pest is the newer side with more to do, but right over the chain bridge is the old town of Buda with the citadel and other elaborate architecture and museums. Climb to the top of Gellert Hill to overlook the entire city and visit the medieval quarter called Castle Hill at the top.

Much of what will interest travelers is on the Buda side. The Castle Hill complex has the Citadel, Fishermen's Fortress, Buda Castle, and an entrance into the catacombs lying just beneath the city. Turkish baths are also popular in Budapest. For the price of a coffee you can get access to a fifteen-minute massage and time spent in the thermal baths. The prices are extremely cheap and depending if you want a facial or a massage depends on what you spend. A slight caution: the baths are not only popular with the tourists, the locals take advantage of the cheap prices and spend long afternoons here as well. Throw your modesty to the side because if you wear any clothes, I can guarantee you will be the only one. I do have to say that I saw way too many old, naked, Hungarian women here. The massage was good though.

On the opposite side of the Danube River is Pest, which has more of a gothic and contemporary feel. The opera house, parliament building and many other monuments are on the eastern side of the city. The major landmark is the stunning Parliament building farther upriver. It is built in the Gothic style and its size is a marvel all on its own.

Also on the Pest side is Hero's Square. This long walk from the riverbank is at the entrance of the city park and has a huge statue in the center of the square.

Around the outsides of this area are more museums and a relaxing promenade into the lesser-crowded areas of Budapest.

For big shoppers, the pedestrian only Váci utca has great deals on antiques, local crafts, trinkets, and even fresh produce. Shopping and dining all over Budapest is relatively inexpensive and stretches a traveler's budge much farther than it would elsewhere in Europe.

The Parliament Building

Hungary is a great place to get a more Eastern feel. The cafés and opera rival those in Vienna, but the inexpensive prices and the fewer crowds come with a trade off. There is little to no English spoken, theft is quite high, and at times I felt the city to be less clean than the wealthier Western capitals. Budapest as well as the rest of Hungary has much to offer, but you must also be willing to give up some of the amenities you may be so accustomed to having.

National Holidays	
January 1	New Year's Day
March 15	Day of the Nation
March/April	Easter Monday
May 1	Labor Day
May/June	Pentecost Monday
August 20	Constitution Day
October 23	Day of the Proclamation of the Republic
October 26	National Day
November 1	All Saints' Day
December 25	Christmas Day
December 26	St. Stephen's Day

Ireland

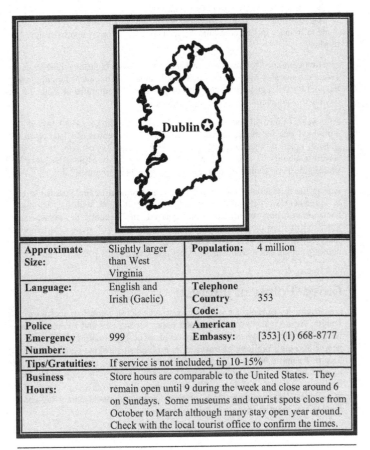

Approximate Size:	Slightly larger than West Virginia	**Population:**	4 million
Language:	English and Irish (Gaelic)	**Telephone Country Code:**	353
Police Emergency Number:	999	**American Embassy:**	[353] (1) 668-8777
Tips/Gratuities:	If service is not included, tip 10-15%		
Business Hours:	Store hours are comparable to the United States. They remain open until 9 during the week and close around 6 on Sundays. Some museums and tourist spots close from October to March although many stay open year around. Check with the local tourist office to confirm the times.		

story and Overview:

Ireland has a long, rich history. Throughout the centuries the island of present day Ireland has been invaded many times and as each invader left they kept behind part of their culture, directly influencing what is now modern day Ireland. Around 100 b.c.e., the arrival of the Celtic people made their way throughout the island. Many years later, St. Patrick made his way throughout the Emerald Isle and converted the pagan people to Christianity. Christianity still plays a crucial role in the Irish way of life and the country's patron saint, St. Patrick, is honored nearly everywhere in Ireland today. In 795 b.c.e. the Vikings invaded 300 years later, eventually setting up camp on the River Liffey, later to become Dublin. Later the Normans invaded. In 1366, the Statutes of Kilkenny forbade Irish/English marriages and prohibited the use of the Irish language, customs and laws. This sparked some of the first issues between the Irish and the English, but in 1649 tensions peaked. After gaining power in England, Oliver Cromwell came to Ireland, sacked cities and reduced the population by approximately two-thirds.

Fighting continued for years and in 1782 the Irish won legislative independence. Times did not stay high for the Irish people though. The potato famine ravaged the country and a good percentage of the population immigrated or died. To this day the low population density is eerily noticeable.

After years of turmoil and to only make things worse, the year 1949 proved to be a troubled year for the Irish. The six northern-most counties of Ulster (Northern Ireland) opted to become Protestant while the remaining counties to the south stayed Catholic. Violence has occurred over this issue for years and Protestantism vs. Catholicism is still a sensitive subject to most Irish.

During the formation of the United Kingdom, Northern Ireland decided to enter in agreement with the British (Scotland, England, and Wales). Through a contentious history of invasions and quarrels, the Republic of Ireland stayed independent from the United Kingdom. The Irish are still quite sensitive when inaccurately lumped into the United Kingdom or Britain. They are proud and patriotic people and to know their history and stance really pleases them.

Cities/Points of Interest:

On arriving to Europe, I knew there was no place I wanted to see more than Dublin. I had many expectations and hopes for the city and I could not have been more pleased when Ireland delivered. The light-hearted attitudes of the people and the simplicity of traveling in an English-speaking country made my time in Ireland a breeze. There is little crime and locals are beyond willing to help. Countless times I would be taking pictures of my friends in front of a landmark and locals would casually walk up and offer to take a picture with all of us in it. This was more the norm than uncommon, and I cannot say enough good things about the people and the country.

Do not be surprised to have many of your stereotypes confirmed when you hear "Danny Boy" being sung by locals in a pub or expletives explode from the mouths of riled up football (our equivalent to soccer and the most popular sport in Europe) fans as their team just lost to its opponent. Double Deckers are everywhere and there are even painted instructions on the roads like, "look left," for the travelers who might get blind sided by a car traveling on the opposite side of the road. Nothing seemed to surprise me while in Ireland, but that is exactly what made it so warm and welcoming.

Dublin

Dublin is clearly the largest and most populated city in Ireland. It is the capital and provides the tourists with more sites and activities in a closer proximity than in the West. The capital city is home to Trinity College, the first European university to grant degrees to women. The university is in the center of town and can be viewed through student-led tours. It is possible to just stroll through the open campus and spend some time in the bookstore and other buildings open to the public. It is in the university bookstore where you will find the Book of Kells. For a small fee you can view the 9th Century illustrated book of the four gospels of the New Testament.

When many hear Ireland, they automatically think about drinking Guinness and an abundance of pubs. Ireland surely will not disappoint. Creator of the dark brewed Guinness Beer, visitors can take a guided tour of the Guinness Storehouse and snap a picture of the famous St. James Gate leading into the brewery. Price of admission includes a self-guided tour and a Guinness at the top of an observation deck. If anything, this tour is worth the view from the top. The panoramic view gives a resounding look over the entire city of Dublin. Try a Guinness in Dublin because locals believe it tastes better than anywhere else in the world. They say it is different because it is brewed with water from the River Liffey, running through downtown which no other brewery can boast.

Pubs are everywhere. Remember that pubs merely sell drinks, while bars include food. Alcohol is very expensive in Dublin, don't be surprised to pay 6€ for a beer. Also remember when asking for a beer, the patron will automatically receive a Guinness.

The Temple Bar District near Trinity's campus is full of pubs, restaurants and traditional Irish music. This is the place to be at night and the place to experience some of the best locals anywhere in Europe.

Temple Bar District, Dublin

For the chance to experience Dublin on your own, get away from the noted tourist sites. Have a picnic at St. Stephen's Green, a huge sprawling park with trees, blooming flowers, ponds and statues everywhere. After relaxing in the city park, take a walk down the city's main drag, O'Connell Street or through the

St. Stephen's Green

pedestrianized Graffton Street. Along the river Liffey are traditional facades of buildings, tiny shops and a great view of the river and the Ha'penny Bridge. There are so many interesting aspects about Dublin that the traditional city sites seem less important.

Dublin is a sprawling city and I ended up spending *a lot* of time walking. Popular sites like the Guinness Storehouse and the notorious Kilmainham Gaol prison are a long and grueling walk. Other sites like the museums, Dublin Castle, Lancaster House and the Remembrance Monument are all within a short distance of one another. Be aware of locations and what you want to see. Dublin has so many places to see and experience that it is important to make sure and see what you came to see. Also, don't forget those walking shoes.

The West

The Western side of Ireland is what most picture when thinking of the lush, green country. Unfortunately, many backpackers do not have the time or resources to view this beautiful countryside. There are some alternatives to seeing such places by going to the city center of Dublin. If you are unable to visit the famous Irish Cliffs of Moher in the West, there are some lesser, though no less-amazing cliffs right outside of Dublin on the coast. Also, St. Stephen's Green gives a comparative feeling to the green and less crowded atmosphere of the west coast.

Public transportation to the Western city's of Galway, Killarny, Cork, Waterford and Shannon are poor. Often times transportation is cut during the wintertime and you may end up getting stranded, like I did, in a desolate city with no real way to get out. Do your research and talk to a tourist office as opposed to locals about how to get to certain places. The best way to travel around Ireland is by car and few of the Dubliners are familiar with the irregularity of western travel through buses and trains.

Ireland is a place that should be a stop on any trip to Europe. The people are the friendliest in Europe, the language barrier is non-existent, and the alternatives between the rolling countryside and the smoky Dublin pubs are entirely up to you. You can make Ireland what you wish. It can be a backpacker's paradise by hopping from town to small town in the west or a great place to party and mingle with the locals in the Temple Bar District. Not enough can be said about Ireland and its people. The only way to know the greatness of Ireland is to experience it for yourself.

National Holidays	
January 1	New Year's Day
March 17	St. Patrick's Day
March/April	Good Friday
March/April	Easter Monday
1st Monday in May	May Bank Holiday
1st Monday in June	June Bank Holiday
1st Monday in August	August Bank Holiday
Last Monday in October	October Bank Holiday
December 25	Christmas Day
December 26	St. Stephen's Day

Italy

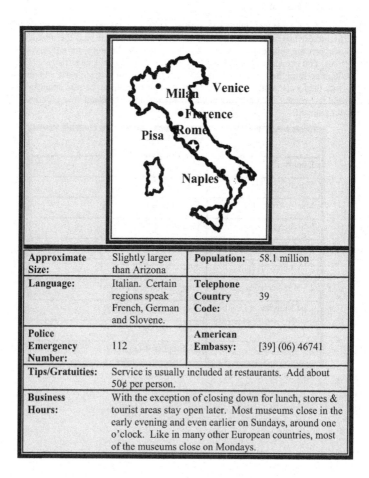

Approximate Size:	Slightly larger than Arizona	Population:	58.1 million
Language:	Italian. Certain regions speak French, German and Slovene.	Telephone Country Code:	39
Police Emergency Number:	112	American Embassy:	[39] (06) 46741
Tips/Gratuities:	Service is usually included at restaurants. Add about 50¢ per person.		
Business Hours:	With the exception of closing down for lunch, stores & tourist areas stay open later. Most museums close in the early evening and even earlier on Sundays, around one o'clock. Like in many other European countries, most of the museums close on Mondays.		

History and Overview:

Much like Greece, Italian history tends to focus on its ancient endeavors and achievements. Around 3000 b.c.e. people started to migrate into the Italian peninsula. The Etruscan federation is formed and exists from around 700-300 b.c.e. These people are known for their love of sex, entertainment, and life in general. The Italian culture today can easily compare itself to its ancient ancestors of nearly 2,500 years ago.

Italy was made up of different states, including powerful Rome, the Papal States, and more diversified regions in the far north and south. The Roman Empire blossomed through military conquests, advancement in its republican-style government and overall prosperity of land acquisition and abundance of slaves to make the Empire more efficient. After the fall of the Empire, Rome went into a major decline until the emergence of the Renaissance.

Between 1300-1400 Italy, mainly Florence, produced some of the most talented artists to ever live. Included among these artisans are: Da Vinci, Raphael, Michelangelo, Boticelli and Giotto. Italy again became a major focus in Europe, trading posts opened in Genoa and Venice, while Milan, Florence, and Rome were credited with art and advancements in science.

Finally in 1861 Rome and the Papal States became part of a unified Italy. Like many other European countries, each of the regions has a different feel. The South is much more laid back and rural, while the North is more focused on industry and high-paced.

Cities/Points of Interest:

If your vacation time is limited and you would like to visit as many notorious places as possible in your short time, Italy is the place to go. Although not my favorite country, it cannot be denied that Italy has some of the best sites and cities in Europe.

Italians embrace the Mediterranean way of life and many seem to be set in their ways. The harsh gesticulations and lack of concern for promptness can be easily confused with rudeness and thus cause an even greater barrier between two cultures. Before traveling to Italy, be sure to expect late trains, long lunches with no open shops, and locals that don't go too much out of their way for tourists.

Many restaurants in Italy charge you to sit down for a meal. It is usually around a 5€ charge. If you want to ditch the fee, there are generally waist-high tables to use instead of sitting. They will never mention the added charges for sitting or for the bread they place on the table. If you are unsure, do your best to ask or scour the menu for the added charges.

Let go of strict schedules and be very open to the possibility of late trains. During my trip to Italy I don't think one train arrived on time. This might be one place to lose the train pass and instead rent a car. Italians drive on the right side of the road and with an International Driver's License and signing a few papers, you can be on your way to discovering Italy on your own terms, and not be vulnerable to the late trains and mess of the areas surrounding the train stations.

The easiest way to travel Italy is by going north to south or vice versa. Start at one end and work your way to the other. From there, catch either a Ryan Air flight or your return flight home.

Venice

Just off the Eastern coast is an island that developed into one of the most influential cities of Europe. Venice remains one of the most expensive and commercial cities on the continent and the obvious attractions bring in droves of tourists.

Venice is best known for its large celebration known as Carnival. This is the time of year I visited and also the same time of the year it seemed everybody else visited. The colorful masks and vibrant music is entertaining but overwhelming. Choose times in the year to avoid this tourism mayhem.

I found Venice to be the most difficult city to navigate. There is no grid design and dissecting the curving streets are winding canals. This island can be extremely frustrating. Keep in mind that you are on an island and you can't get off. Note that at each intersection there should be a sign pointing you to the closest landmark. Use this and whatever map skills you have to navigate the interconnecting streets.

Perhaps the best way to get around Venice, other than walking, is by taking advantage of its many water transportation services. The city is known for its gondolas, but these long boats accompanied by singing gondoliers are overdone and expensive. By sacrificing a little of the stereotypical Venetian water ride

experience, use a bus boat or ferry to cross the canals to get to a popular spot. The locals and only the savviest of travelers primarily use these modes of transportation.

As I stated, Venice is very expensive and often very crowded. Finding a room is difficult and sometimes unsuccessful. Either plan early or make a stop at the tourist office and use their services to help locate a room for the night. Staying in a neighboring town on the mainland also saves money and confusion.

The primary place to see while in Venice is St. Mark's Square. This public square is home to St. Mark's Basillica, the world's first digital clock, the Ducal Palace and the Campanile. This pigeon haven is packed with tourists and crowded during the afternoon. Visit here early, see the magnificent buildings and take an elevator to the top of the Campanile and look at the view of Venice beneath you.

Walking through the alleys and taking ferries may make you feel nervous about the possibility of getting lost. Ignore those fears and wander aimlessly until you find a recognizable landmark or a helpful local. It is those undiscovered squares and storefront canals that Venice was originally about.

Rialto Bridge, Venice

From Venice there are tiny islands located in the lagoon, each known for their own handicrafts. Ferries leave for Torcello, Burana, and Murano regularly making it easy to get away from the craziness of Venice in the afternoon.

Florence

As the capital of Tuscany, Florence has produced some of the best artists the world has ever seen. Michelangelo, DaVinci, Raphael, and others have learned, lived, and produced art that is still studied and revered today.

Florence is a relatively small city with a layout easy to navigate. The best way to get around is by foot. There are a number of American schools and American influences in Florence and it seemed as though I heard more English than Italian. You will have no problem getting around and no problem communicating with the locals here.

To appreciate Florence and to gain the most from it, I feel it is important to understand the Renaissance and comprehend the figures that made up this influential period in history. Every facet of the city devotes itself to the 12th century. If your main focus in Florence is the museums and artwork, plan your trip for off-season to avoid the lines.

Nearly all that you will be interested in seeing is on the North Bank of the Arno. The South Bank has a few public squares and cathedrals that are worth seeing, but the more notable sites are on the opposite side of the river.

Lines start early for all of the sites and you will inevitably be waiting in crowds. The museums are phenomenal for those who enjoy Renaissance and primarily Italian art. The Uffizi is the most popular with works from Botticelli, da Vinci, and others. The art I have learned about for years in textbooks I could finally inspect up close. I was slightly disappointed by the limited selection and was much more pleasantly surprised by the Academia, which is farther to the north. This art gallery has the original "David" created by Michelangelo himself. The other sculptures and pieces were extraordinary.

My first stop in Florence was the Duomo and Baptistery. It is important to see these early because, like everywhere in Florence, the lines are long. A cheap fee gives you a pass to walk through the inner-workings of the cathedral, walk around the base of the dome, and climb to the roof to get the best view of Florence anywhere. This hefty hike is not for the faint-hearted or even slightly claustrophobic. I found myself stuck between two others in a hallway meant for only one person. The walkways are closed in and fresh air seems to be at a

View from atop the Duomo

premium. Although the walk was strenuous and a few anxiety attacks were faced, the view from the top and the opportunity to let my feet dangle and take in Florence was worth the fee and the fear of climbing in the close quarters of the Duomo.

Right next door to the Duomo is the Baptistery, another amazing building constructed during the Renaissance. Aside from the beautiful colors adorning the Baptistery, it is the doors that receive the most attention. Now replicas, Ghiberti's "Gates of Paradise" is a mouth dropping, gold plated piece of art. The precision and creativity put into the doors of the Baptistery are amazing and worth seeing.

For a nice break stop in a local gelato shop. Gelato is Italian ice cream and easily the best ice cream you will ever eat. There is no telling how many calories are in each scoop, but the flavor and ambiance of eating gelato on a Florentine sidewalk is worth the few pounds.

Florence is a shopper's paradise. There are a number of flea markets containing everything from scarves to antiques. The booths give good deals and are a great place to pick up some souvenirs or gifts for those back home. Upscale shopping can be found in one of the hundreds of boutiques and larger stores. Also, the bridge stratling the Arno River known as the Ponte Vechio is lined with primarily jewelry shops among other novelties. It is impossible to leave Florence without buying something. Mark out some time to mingle with the locals and to buy local crafts.

Pisa

Pisa is only a short hour to an hour and a half train ride from Florence. I had an afternoon open so I hopped on the first train and went to Pisa for the day. Note that there is very little to do in the town except to see its famous Leaning Tower. Crime seemed to be high and once you stray away from the main tourist paths, you give up much of the security of safety in numbers.

Leaning Tower Complex - Pisa, Italy

The Tower Complex not only has the tower, but a cathedral and baptistery as well. Visitors can climb to the top of the Tower, view the inside of the cathedral, or walk the grounds to take those ever-so-famous pictures of you holding the tower up with your hands.

Running alongside the complex are shops, vendors, and restaurants. Women especially get barraged with offers from vendors. Keep your distance and continue walking unless you plan to stop in the shops or negotiate with a street seller. A nice early dinner is a great way to leave the crowded tours and noise of other travelers. Most of the restaurants have seating outside with an ideal view of the Leaning Tower. I nibbled on pasta, drank some wine, and took in the beautiful surroundings.

Rome

On yet another late train from Pisa to Rome, the hour and a half ride took nearly five. After finishing another book I stepped off the train in Rome. The smog coupled with the number of people and Vespas was a little overwhelming. Once on the back streets the comfort level assumed a normal position. It is pointless to list each of the amazing sites to see in Rome. Everyone knows to see the Coliseum and the Forum. Every map and sign in the city points to another historic landmark.

My advice for Rome is to give yourself ample time to see and do everything. It is a huge city and it takes a lot of time to walk around. Block out an entire day for the Vatican. Lines there can be longer than anywhere else in Europe. Expect

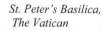

Tiber River linking Rome to the Vatican.

The Forum

St. Peter's Basilica, The Vatican

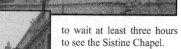

to wait at least three hours to see the Sistine Chapel.

Each site needs its own, individual attention. Take one day to visit the northern part of the city with Piazza Navona, the Pantheon, Trevi fountains, the Spanish Steps and much more. You will become extremely exhausted if you push too hard without getting a full feel for the city. The summer heat can be draining and the exhaust from all of the cars makes it that much worse.

Beware of rain that is dirt. During my time in Rome I experienced dirt falling from the sky. Locals informed me that the sand from the Sahara is picked up into the clouds and occasionally rains down on parts of Italy. It ruined my clothes and made for a very frustrating afternoon. Have back up plans. Duck into a museum or grab a bite at a local café to avoid this added burden.

Naples

From Rome I hopped a train to Naples. Upon stepping onto the platform, I quickly felt uncomfortable. There were men fighting, people breaking into pay phones for the change, and the train station appeared to be a Holiday Inn for the homeless. Police officers kept chatting and locals walked right past everything as though nothing was happening. I felt my security and health at risk. I later found out that it is unwise for tourists to travel in southern Italy, especially Naples in the winter. Safety in numbers is the way to escape this rather crime-ridden area. If Naples is a stop on your itinerary, either be extremely prepared, or plan your trip during the time of heavy tourism, April-October.

Visiting Naples gives tourists a great outlet to see some spectacular sites. A quick train ride to the south is the city of Pompeii that was demolished after the eruption of Mt. Vesuvius. Visitors can see artifacts that survived or people covered in ash, killed the instant the volcano hit them. For any history lover this is a must-see, and I do suggest that all go to visit if given the time.

Another favorite for tourists is the island of Capri. A ferry ride from Naples drops guests off on a lush and beautiful island. It is touristy but this excursion diverts from Naples and the even more densely populated areas.

Although I had some difficult times in Italy, I still highly recommend it for travelers visiting Europe. It has over five major cities to give visitors exactly what they are looking for, and the countryside seems as though no tourist has ever discovered it. You can get the best of both worlds here, big city hustle and bustle and the laid back, Mediterranean attitude of the countryside. Art, culture, and history abound, catering to each travelers' individual likes and dislikes. Italy dominates a great deal of time to visit all of it, so plan accordingly and take in one of the oldest civilizations in Europe.

National Holidays	
January 1	New Year's Day
January 6	Epiphany
March/April	Easter Monday
April 25	Liberation Day 1945
May 1	Labor Day
June 2	Anniversary of the Republic
August 15	Assumption of the Virgin
November 1	All Saints' Day
December 8	Immaculate Conception
December 25	Christmas Day
December 26	St. Stephen's Day

Luxembourg

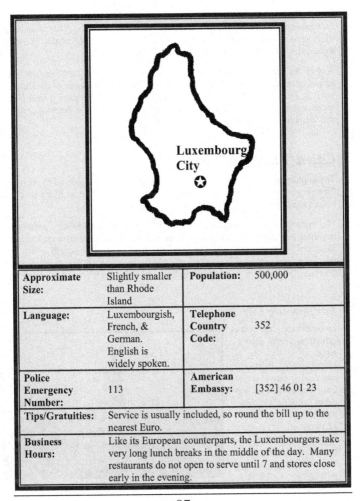

Approximate Size:	Slightly smaller than Rhode Island	Population:	500,000
Language:	Luxembourgish, French, & German. English is widely spoken.	Telephone Country Code:	352
Police Emergency Number:	113	American Embassy:	[352] 46 01 23
Tips/Gratuities:	Service is usually included, so round the bill up to the nearest Euro.		
Business Hours:	Like its European counterparts, the Luxembourgers take very long lunch breaks in the middle of the day. Many restaurants do not open to serve until 7 and stores close early in the evening.		

History and Overview:

The tiny country of Luxembourg has spent most of its existence changing rulers, changing languages, and changing governments. In 963, Luxembourg City was established when Count Siegfried built a castle atop one of the ravines. About four hundred years later Luxembourg was named a Grand Duchy and to this day remains as the only one in the world.

After Napoleon's defeat at Waterloo in 1815, The Congress of Vienna formed the Kingdom of the Netherlands, which included the Netherlands, Belgium and Luxembourg. Luxembourg took on many influences from the other nations and the flag is strikingly similar to the Dutch flag, the only difference being the lighter shade of blue.

Within the same century Luxembourg gained its independence but was soon forced onto the front lines of both World Wars, hosting the Battle of the Bulge as well as some other famous battles. The United States liberated Luxembourg twice and for that reason, most Luxembourgers appear to be eternally grateful and welcoming to Americans.

Cities/Points of Interest:

The country of Luxembourg is extremely small and often neglected by travelers. This is where I lived while in Europe and I find it to be a great home base and place to spend a couple of relaxing days.

The culture is diverse and Lux borrows a lot from its neighbors. Luxembourg has three languages: French spoken in the South and West, German spoken in the East, and Luxembourgish all over as the national language. English is also very prominent and spoken often. If you are able to speak any of these four languages you should have no problem traveling throughout the small country.

Luxembourg City

Luxembourg City is the capital and only decent-sized city in Luxembourg. It has the country's only major train station and a bus depot willing to take travelers anywhere. Luxembourg is a great home base because Europe's major cities are within a close proximity. Brussels is

three hours away, Paris is three and a half, Frankfurt is four, Zurich is five, and London is six. Like in most major cities, the area around the train stations can become fairly dangerous at night. The same goes for Luxembourg. Although this central European country has the highest per capita income rate in the world and the crime rate is low, drug dealers and prostitutes tend to congregate near the train station at night.

Taking a right out of the train station, points you down a long road lined with shops and eventually depositing you in the Vielle Ville, or old town. In this district and nearby are the Royal Palace of the Grand Duchy, open pedestrian squares and the City Hall. Also within walking distance is the International Court of Justice for the European Union and adjacent to it are other museums and the Cathédrale de Notre-Dame.

Luxembourg City is built upon the ravines of the Alzette and Pétrusse Rivers. Below the cliffs is the Grund. This area has most of the neighborhoods and nightlife of the city. Pubs and bars flourish in the cozy area and it is not hard to find college aged kids walking the streets to find the next bar.

A Bridge over The Grund

This town has a lot to offer once you get away from the downtown, noisy atmosphere next to the train station. Stop at the high-end boutiques on the way to the pedestrian squares, visit the old parts of the city and then my favorite area, the Grund.

Luxembourg City is the only place to really experience a city-like feel in the country, but the outer-lying regions are great places to visit. To take a train from the extreme south of Luxembourg to the northern tip is only 45 minutes. The country is small and easily navigable. Trains run smoothly but to some of the smaller towns, they do not visit as regularly.

The South is more industrial and less necessary to visit. Just outside of the City are military cemeteries in Hamm honoring those lost on the front lines of the World Wars. Here you can visit General George Patton's grave, which is always adorned with flowers and U.S. flags.

To the north is the town of Clervaux and its highlight, the Abbey. Here, I attended an open vesper service and for even the least spiritual the hymns of the monks are all too inspiring and incredible.

The area that will cost you the most film is the West. The Battle of the Bulge was fought in the northwestern town of Diekirch and military museums and battlefields are clearly marked. Just a few miles north is Vianden Castle. This medieval castle is open to the public and the view from the top overlooks the Valley of the Our on the border with Germany.

Vianden Castle

And finally, for a relaxing afternoon visit the Moselle Valley in the west. This border with Germany has some of the best small towns in Luxembourg and has a large amount of vineyards. The area is known for its wine, so take an afternoon to stroll the vineyards and sample the different types of wine produced.

Although very small with only a few tourist attractions, Luxembourg is well worth the stop. The countryside is beautiful and the capital city is a simple town to rest-up and use as a home base. Even the most amateur of travelers can find their way around Luxembourg and use their minimal language skills to interact with the locals. The low crime rate and the high-income rate of this country make it safe to enjoy.

National Holidays	
January 1	New Year's Day
February/March	Carnival Day
March/April	Easter Monday
May 1	Labor Day
May/June	Ascension Day
May/June	Pentecost Monday
June 23	National Day
1st Monday in September	Luxembourg City Fête (In Luxembourg City, only)
November 1	All Saints' Day
December 25	Christmas Day
December 26	St. Stephen's Day

The Netherlands

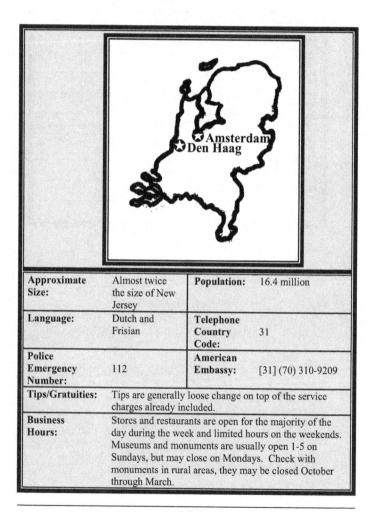

Approximate Size:	Almost twice the size of New Jersey	Population:	16.4 million
Language:	Dutch and Frisian	Telephone Country Code:	31
Police Emergency Number:	112	American Embassy:	[31] (70) 310-9209
Tips/Gratuities:	Tips are generally loose change on top of the service charges already included.		
Business Hours:	Stores and restaurants are open for the majority of the day during the week and limited hours on the weekends. Museums and monuments are usually open 1-5 on Sundays, but may close on Mondays. Check with monuments in rural areas, they may be closed October through March.		

History and Overview:

The Holy Roman Empire extended as far north as the Netherlands on continental Europe. Germanic and Celtic tribes lived alongside the Romans and after Spaniard, Charles V was named Holy Roman Emperor the Dutch were soon under Spanish rule.

The Spanish push for Catholicism was stopped during the Counter-Reformation and the Dutch became Protestant. Shortly thereafter the small country made an attempt to centralize the government which led to a revolt against Spain. On July 26, 1581, the Netherlands gained independence.

Following independence the Netherlands went through a Golden Age. The formation of the Dutch East India Company made Amsterdam a major trading city and the heart of the Netherlands. Science, trade, and art all made advances during this time as well.

One problem that has always plagued the Dutch has been its ever-going process of reclaiming land. Amsterdam today sits ten feet below sea level. Dams, movable barriers, and dykes hold back water and give the Dutch an opportunity to dry up the areas originally covered with water, to gain land that once sat beneath it. Land is precious to the Dutch and vast amounts have been reclaimed from the sea in the last 60 years. If you visit, you will notice that buildings are built more vertical as opposed to horizontal, every piece of land is being utilized to its full potential even down to a personal level. You will notice the Dutch stand much closer to one another than we do in the United States.

Cities/Points of Interest:

A popular destination for many college-aged travelers is the Netherlands, and more particularly Amsterdam. This is due to the liberal nature and easy accessibility to drugs and other vices. There is much more to see in The Netherlands than Amsterdam and I suggest breaking away from the often crowded and over-indulged city for the Dutch countryside and the other major cities.

Many refer to The Netherlands as Holland, but this name really only refers to the Western Provinces that are home to the most populated cities: Rotterdam, Amsterdam and The Hague. This small country is the most densely populated in the Europe and while visiting inside these cities, this statistic is quickly apparent.

Land is very valuable to the Dutch and as a result, the intense land reclamation projects have become a major foucs. Every stretch of land is important to the locals and the great moisture in the land has given The Netherlands a rolling, lush green countryside that is hard to match elsewhere in Europe. Visit during the spring time, and you will likely see what the Dutch are best known for; their wide array of tulips and other flowers.

Amsterdam

Easily the most liberal city in Holland and probably in Europe, Amsterdam is extremely popular among younger crowds. With Amsterdam, what you see is what you get. Expect to see prostitutes in the Red Light District, "Coffee Shops" lining every street, and uncomfortable public displays of affection are widely seen.

In the time I stayed in Amsterdam I was offered more drugs and tickets to live sex shows than I could have possibly imagined. There is a large abundance of marijuana sellers and shops eager to sell to young tourists. I would not consider myself a prude, but Amsterdam seemed to be more "in your face" and almost too much.

The Red Light District

Instead of spending my time in Amsterdam in a foggy haze, I opted to see the sites (most of my friends back home couldn't believe it, and hated me for wasting my golden opportunity of marijuana legalization for site-seeing). Nonetheless, my attention was focused on the more traditional and low-key sites of Amsterdam.

The city is set up in a semi-circular shape with a multitude of canals lacing between the streets. The easiest way to see everything is to plot out what you want to see and make a circular route around the city. I chose to start off with the places that tend to have the longest lines.

The Anne Frank House is a poignant and must-see stop. Lines start early and the small annex is difficult to navigate through crowds, so start early. After an hour or so of touring, reading entries, and watching short films, my travel partners and I moved on to our next stop: the Sex Museum. Yes, it did feel quite awkward visiting a historical and emotional site then moving onto a museum showing centuries of pornography and displays.

There are multiple sex museums in Amsterdam. Be sure to read up on each of them to decide which one is most closely aligned with what you want to see. There is a museum that takes a more historical look at how sex has blossomed over the history of the world, and then there is the one more graphic museum that has entire rooms dedicated to photos of bestiality and porns made from the 19th century. Be wary and be open if you will be visiting either a sex museum or live sex show. Americans are more conservative and regard talking of sex as a taboo which is in sharp contrast with Europeans. Be prepared to feel voyeuristic, uncomfortable, and slightly tainted after you visit these, "no holds bar" places.

After grabbing a quick lunch and hitting up some shops, the next most logical place to visit was the Red Light District. Sex shops, coffee shops and outdoor toilets are everywhere. Don't be surprised to see women sitting in windows as well as prostitutes on the streets. At night this area gets quite dangerous, so when looking for a hostel try to find one not in the heart of sex, drugs, and alcohol. Another word to the wise: DO NOT take pictures of the prostitutes. If you are seen doing so, you will be arrested and fined.

The Heineken Brewery is a bargain and a great stop just on the outside of the ring surrounding the main part of the city. For just €7 the price of entry, an interactive tour of the brewery, three draughts of Heineken and a souvenir glass with tin are included. You can also record a short video that can be emailed to your friends and family. This is one of the cheapest and most fun places to take a break and drink some beer for a good price.

Amsterdam is home to two of the greatest painters and a variety of different museums. Spend time wandering through historical museums or the two top museums in Amsterdam: The Van Gogh Museum and the Rembrandt Museum. Both hold the works of the painting legends and act as a counter to the more "sexy" attractions.

Adjacent to the Van Gogh Museum is Amsterdam's primary city park, Vondelpark. Inside this area are public skating rinks in the wintertime, rose gardens, film societies and other unexpected attractions. Not long after spending some time walking the sidewalks and watching the locals, I quickly forgot I was in the uber-crowded city of Amsterdam.

This book does not have the typical recommendations for accommodations or restaurants, but one place I will note is the Stay Ok Vondelpark Hostel close to the city park. Hostels are very hit or miss and it is hard to know what to expect until you are there. Follow some of my advice from the "Accommodations" chapter to increase your chances of finding a hostel closest to your expectations. Stay Ok Vondelpark is outside the craziness of the city, but still within a close walk and provides a cheap rate, big rooms, private showers, clean sheets and breakfast which includes a sizeable selection of food. Internet access and the help of the staff make this hostel one of the best in Europe for the price.

Another lesson I learned while in Amsterdam: be prepared to have tricks played on you by locals. Many young (especially American) tourists sometimes end up the butt of a joke by entertained locals. When my girlfriends and I asked for a recommendation of a club or bar to visit while in Amsterdam, we got a resounding answer to attend "Paradiso." With the enthusiasm of all around us, we thought it would be a great idea to have a night on the town. After paying the hefty cover and getting frisked by a rather friendly bouncer we were all admitted into the club. It did not take long to notice, however, that there were no girls dancing with guys and vice-versa. The locals teasingly pointed us in the direction of a gay dance club. Although it was very unexpected and not what I was used to, the fun loving nature of the Dutch and the up-tempo techno music still made the night one never to forget.

Den Haag

This royal capital of The Netherlands has a distinctly important feel. Mainly referred to by its English name, The Hague is also home to international organizations and other royal buildings that make their residence in this third-largest city of The Netherlands.

Den Haag, like Rotterdam, has a more metropolitan feel. There is little to do in The Hague unless you want to explore the stately buildings of the Peace Palace, Binnenhof or other Municipal museums. As a short stop on my way from Amsterdam, Den Haag was a great afternoon jaunt. Also close by is the quaint town of Delft, known for it's blue and white porcelain crafts.

I urge you, as in most of the other European countries, to break away from the over-crowded and often chaotic big cities. For a first time trip or for a limited amount of days the big cities are great to enjoy. If there is extra time and you feel more comfortable traveling off the beaten path, it is likely you will experience and see more than you might imagine.

National Holidays	
January 1	New Year's Day
March/April	Good Friday
March/April	Easter Monday
April 30	Queen's Birthday
May 5	Liberation Day (occurs every 5 years; next in 2009)
May/June	Ascension Day
May/June	Pentecost Monday
December 25	Christmas Day
December 26	St. Stephen's Day

Norway

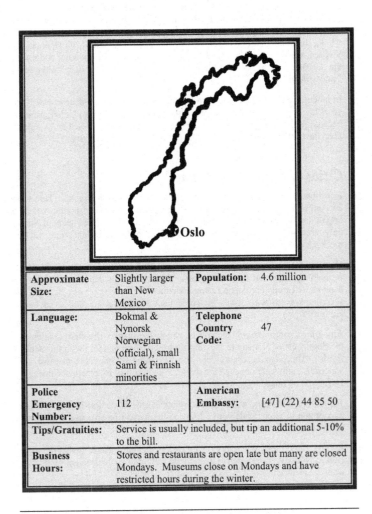

Approximate Size:	Slightly larger than New Mexico	**Population:**	4.6 million
Language:	Bokmal & Nynorsk Norwegian (official), small Sami & Finnish minorities	**Telephone Country Code:**	47
Police Emergency Number:	112	**American Embassy:**	[47] (22) 44 85 50
Tips/Gratuities:	Service is usually included, but tip an additional 5-10% to the bill.		
Business Hours:	Stores and restaurants are open late but many are closed Mondays. Museums close on Mondays and have restricted hours during the winter.		

History and Overview:

The Vikings dominate Norwegian history. From 800-1050 they sailed the seas, pillaged towns, raided villages and ventured as far west as North America. The interaction with other neighbors and the loot gained from conquests boosted the economy and made the Vikings a very powerful group of people.

Within one hundred years King Harald I united much of Norway and less than a century after that, all citizens were forced to convert to Christianity. Following the decline of the Vikings, the Plague ravaged Norway resulting in nearly half of the population dead. This devastated the economy and weakened the state as a whole. In an attempt to recover, Norway entered into a union with Denmark and Sweden, which eventually ceded Norway to Sweden. Like the other countries in the Union, Norway accepted the Reformation and the people converted to Protestantism.

In modern times, Norway played a big role as a founding member of NATO but years later rejected offers to become a member in the European Union; primarily because Norway began extracting oil and gas from the North Sea and wanted to keep the profits to themselves in order to further build the country.

Cities/Points of Interest:

Unfortunately I spent very little time in this Scandinavian country. Due to the ever-present mix up of train times, I spent only a couple of hours in Oslo as opposed to the ten that I had planned. However, the short time I spent in Norway only strengthened my desire to revisit the land of beautiful landscape and even nicer people.

Norway thrives on tradition and that is what makes up the resilient and welcoming culture of the Norwegians. Souvenir shops depict the history with hand carved trolls and Viking paraphernalia. The local traditions and folk tales shed light as to why locals welcome their harsh weather and even harsher landscape.

Along the western coast is the area known as Fjordland. The coast leading from the Southwest of Norway to the very tip in the North is inlaid with thousands of fjords. This area in unforgiving and has some of the most massive cliffs, waterfalls, and water coves in the world. The best way to experience this part of Norway is by boat.

To venture into some of the more remote places of central Norway, it is not uncommon to hitch a ride with a local postman and ride around the countryside to areas most tourists never see.

A photo opportunity that many joking college students take is to visit the town of Hell in Norway. Located near Trondheim and quite difficult to get to, many just want the chance to say they have been to "Hell and back."

Lillehammer just north of Oslo, was home to the 1994 winter Olympic Games with the Olympic park and other sites commemorating the world games.

Oslo

The weather is brutal and getting around this Scandinavian country can be difficult, so most tourists stick to visiting Norway's capital, Oslo. The recommended way to enter Oslo is by boat into the magnificent harbor of Oslofjorden. I, however, entered into Oslo via a train from Stockholm that took only five hours. The train ride alone was worth the money and time. I arrived at the city's train station and was greeted by a welcoming committee of train station workers giving the female passengers (and my left-out male friend) a rose for Valentine's Day.

The feeling of cleanliness and serenity only surmounted the crisp air of the February day. The streets were not crowded, English was prevalent, and the people were always willing to help.

Royal Palace, Oslo

Oslo is easily seen by foot, but the public transportation is highly organized and also a great way to make quick excursions. Once exiting the train station, Karl Johans Gate is just a short walk. This avenue leads visitors to see some of the city's most important sites, such as the Oslo Cathedral and the Parliament building. Visiting the harbor is beautiful and definitely worth taking pictures. Along the water's edge are even more places of interest.

Oslo, like every other capital city, has a national gallery and other museums including the Munch Museum that is home to Edvard Munch's famous painting,

The Scream. The Royal Palace is easily accessible and poses for a great photograph. Other popular sites include the city hall and the city's most famous stop, Vigeland Park. Upscale shopping abounds and there is no shortage on places to browse, whether they are high-end boutiques or family run souvenir shops.

Norway is a country that exudes openness, in its untouched expanse of land or in its peoples' liberal attitudes toward outsiders. Norwegians make all who visit feel welcome and they give the usual hectic and high-stressed European vacation a relaxed and invigorating reprieve.

National Holidays	
January 1	New Year's Day
March/April	Maundy Thursday
March/April	Good Friday
March/April	Easter Monday
May	Ascension Day
May 1	Labor Day
May 17	National Day
May/June	Pentecost Monday
December 25	Christmas Day
December 26	St. Stephen's Day

Poland

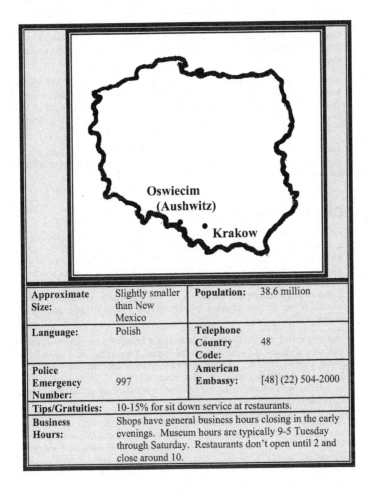

Approximate Size:	Slightly smaller than New Mexico	Population:	38.6 million
Language:	Polish	Telephone Country Code:	48
Police Emergency Number:	997	American Embassy:	[48] (22) 504-2000
Tips/Gratuities:	10-15% for sit down service at restaurants.		
Business Hours:	Shops have general business hours closing in the early evenings. Museum hours are typically 9-5 Tuesday through Saturday. Restaurants don't open until 2 and close around 10.		

History and Overview:

Poland is another country in which the majority of its studied history is within the past one hundred years. Russian invasions and two World Wars have expanded and lessened the amount of Polish land holdings over time.

In 966, the Polish Nation was formally recognized and Duke Mieszke is regarded as the first leader. His marriage to a Catholic Bohemian princess directly resulted in his personal conversion as well as the ultimate order for all Poles to convert to Catholicism. This union plays a strong role in Polish history and daily life because to this day, Poland is the most actively participating Catholic nation. Over 90% of the residents practice regularly by going to church or other Catholic practices. Churches are abundant and on Sundays, the majority of the country is shut down.

After a string of Mongol invasions, years of independence, and military battlegrounds, the Congress of Vienna in 1815 put Poland under Russian control. Poles were persecuted and Russian laws and practices were enforced in many areas. Leadership transferred during the World Wars but from 1946-1950, Poland was used as a Soviet Satellite to broaden Communism.

Today Poland seems to have a reserved personality and a strong faith after the years of Russian occupation and communism. The times of Russian influence did little to change the core of the Polish people.

Cities/Points of Interest:

An often forgotten and misunderstood country, Poland has the possibility to become a more noticed stop on the European travelers' radar. Purely out of a whim and a desire to see the less traveled, my friends and I rode into the southern city of Krakow. The country's capital of Warsaw is more famous and more historically significant due to the attention and unfortunate circumstances brought upon it during the World Wars. The South, however, is less damaged and seems to be less affected by the ravages of Soviet rule and German destruction.

Our train rolled into the Krakow train station at four in the morning to a candlelit and eerie silence. Walking through the station, I remember thinking to myself "what a nice ambiance." I found out only minutes later that the entire city of Krakow was without electricity. This meant that no lockers were available, no streetlights were on and more importantly no ATMs were operating to retrieve local currency.

The general plan was to store our bags in a locker and get onto the first tour of Auschwitz in the morning. Unfortunately we could not pay the operators in cash because we had no local currency and the electronic lockers were inoperable. Thankfully, within the hour the electricity was back on and all was well. It did not take long to figure out, though, that the bus station is where the homeless slept. I was heckled by women asking for money and men with no teeth mumbling things in Polish, which I'm sure I didn't want to understand. Shortly thereafter a man that had to be over 6 foot tall, crawled out of what looked to be his home, a nearby locker.

My first hour in Poland was a complete culture shock, but in no way did it foreshadow what was to come. I was about to board a tour bus to the concentration camp of Auschwitz nearly two hours away and see what are probably the most profound memories I obtained while in Europe.

Gate at Auschwitz Concentration Camp

The English-led tour of Auschwitz took small groups through the barracks, work camps, and crematorium. There are no words to describe the emotions evoked by the sites we saw. After the Auschwitz part of the tour, a bus led us to Birknau that was essentially the extermination part of the camp and the site where Steven Spielburg shot *Schindler's List*. Although emotionally trying, this tour was astounding and absolutely worth taking.

After regrouping from the tour, I could enjoy the bus ride back through the surprisingly beautiful Polish countryside. It is very reminiscent of its western neighbor, Germany with the rolling hills, rivers and green trees.

Krakow

As in most cities, the areas around the train and bus stations are the highest in crime and the least attractive parts of a city. After the scare that morning with no electricity and my encounters with homeless beggars, I was not looking forward to returning back to Krakow. We got back to town and headed right for the historic center and the town square. Here you can view the Jewish sectors and the dominating fortress in the city park. The easy stroll around the park eventually dumped us into the winding streets of the city center. Taking in my surroundings I thought that here was a town that truly shows you cannot judge a city based on the area surrounding its train station. Krakow is a lovely city.

The center part of Krakow has countless shops, restaurants and unexpected sites. There was a flea market in the middle of the square with beautiful chess boards and cloths. Restaurants are extremely inexpensive and well serviced. I recall having one of my best meals, 4 courses, for about 4€. Nearly all restaurants in Europe post their menu and prices outside by the door. Check before entering to see if the meal will be within budget and what your palate may want for the day.

Although the North has more historical significance and more landscape to cover, I felt fulfilled by only venturing into the South. The small-town feel of Krakow and the bus tour to Auschwitz did not force me to attempt Polish or make me feel overwhelmed. The much-enjoyed short trip was unexpected yet welcomed as I boarded the train again to head off for another destination.

National Holidays	
January 1	New Year's Day
March/April	Easter Monday
May 1	May Day
May 3	Constitution Day
June 15	Corpus Christi
November 1	All Saints' Day
November 11	Independence Day
December 25	Christmas Day

Portugal

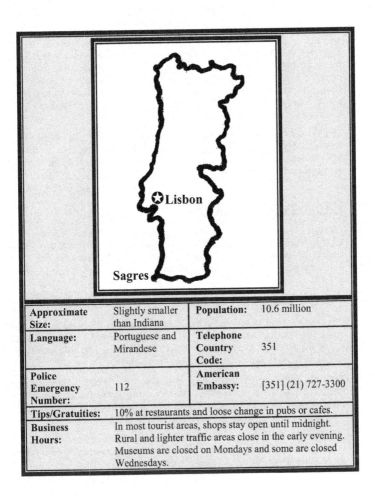

Approximate Size:	Slightly smaller than Indiana	**Population:**	10.6 million
Language:	Portuguese and Mirandese	**Telephone Country Code:**	351
Police Emergency Number:	112	**American Embassy:**	[351] (21) 727-3300
Tips/Gratuities:	10% at restaurants and loose change in pubs or cafes.		
Business Hours:	In most tourist areas, shops stay open until midnight. Rural and lighter traffic areas close in the early evening. Museums are closed on Mondays and some are closed Wednesdays.		

History and Overview:

Living in relative harmony, the Celts, Visigoths, Romans, Phoenicians, and Carthaginians occupied what is present-day Portugal. It was in 711 when the Muslim North Africans, known as the Moors invaded the Iberian Peninsula. They spread all throughout Spain and up the Atlantic coast through Portugal. Resistance was high, but strongest in the northernmost regions. These areas held off the Moorish invaders and kept their land. This is the reason why Portugal does not expand the entire length of the western coast of the Iberian Peninsula. The northern part of the west coast remains a Spanish territory.

The Age of Discovery was an important time for the Portuguese. In the 16th century, Portugal utilized its strong navy and navigation systems to be the first to round the Cape of Good Hope in Africa, settling in Eastern Africa and other places. The Portuguese were also the first to reach the country of Brazil. The King's son was sent to rule the newly founded country. It was then, that the natives were forced to adopt Portuguese as their new language and engage in many relations with Portugal.

This Golden Age ended when Portugal was invaded by Spain. Its isolation from Europe and close interaction with its neighbor has given Portugal a sense of individualism. Its people see their culture different from that of Spain's and are not as regularly bombarded by tourists.

Cities/Points of Interest:

Portugal is a country often overlooked by many tourists. It is not geographically close to other tourist hot spots, so many tend to put it off, and stick to the more centralized locations. I only spent a minimal amount of time here, but I was quite surprised to have found such a gorgeous country.

Lisbon and Porto

The capital city of Lisbon and the second largest city of Porto are definite tour attractions with their old-fashioned and less modernized feel. Visiting Portugal is like stepping back in time and the cities are dominated more by centuries old buildings, rather than new international business offices.

Porto lies in the north of the country, just on the Atlantic coast. Famous for its wine, Porto also is a large producer of cork. This is one place I recommend taking a tour of a distillery or winery. It is possible that this unique Portuguese wine could convert even the most biased Bordeaux lovers.

Although Porto is the second largest city in Portugal it can easily be toured in a couple short days. Enjoy the narrow streets and the old buildings to gain a better appreciation of the Portuguese culture and history.

The capital of Portugal known as Lisboa to the locals is the hub of Portuguese activities. The small coastal country only has two major cities and the rest of the countryside is dotted with much smaller towns and villages.

Portuguese is a very difficult language to speak or to comprehend, so it is best to learn a few key phrases before traveling. If you are educated in Spanish, it may be possible to read the language, but in no way are the Portuguese accepting of visitors assuming they are the same language. Lisbon and Porto are large cities so English may not be too difficult to find, however, once you step out of the comfort zone of the major cities, English is scarce.

Lisbon can also be toured by foot to most of its sites; however, the most famous attraction in the capital city, Belém Tower, lies just outside the city and needs a bus or tram to locate. Also, take a quick half hour train ride to the town of Cabo da Roca and stand on the Western most point of continental Europe.

The architecture and the nostalgic European ambiance are worth the trip to Portugal. In the midst of wandering the streets and buying handcrafted souvenir tiles, you can't help but feel like you are in a truly exotic place.

The Algarve

Growing in popularity and the place where I spent my time, the Algarve coast is now flourishing with tourists. Taking a drive along the highway in the south leads you along a blissfully peaceful route of small villages and locals doing everyday chores, such as hanging their clothes to dry. Everything from the open fields to the smell in the air is enchanting.

The highway ends at Sagres, the southwestern most point of Portugal. Here visitors can stand overlooking the steep cliffs and the thrashing ocean hitting upon the jagged rocks. Atop the hill, where the Atlantic meets the Mediterranean, is the School of Navigation fittingly built by Henry the Navigator five hundred years ago.

Sagres, Portugal

Stop at a family-owned restaurant and dine on the tasty seafood and wine. This day trip presents the chance to take the open road into your own hands and move at your own pace without the pressure of the big cities. Relax, enjoy, and take in the beauty southern Portugal has to offer.

National Holidays	
January 1	New Year's Day
February/March	Shrove Tuesday
March/April	Good Friday
March/April	Easter Monday
April 25	Liberty Day
May 1	Labor Day
May/June	Corpus Christi
June 10	Portugal Day
August 15	Assumption of the Virgin
October 5	Republic Day
November 1	All Saints' Day
December 1	Independence Day
December 8	Immaculate Conception
December 25	Christmas Day

Scotland

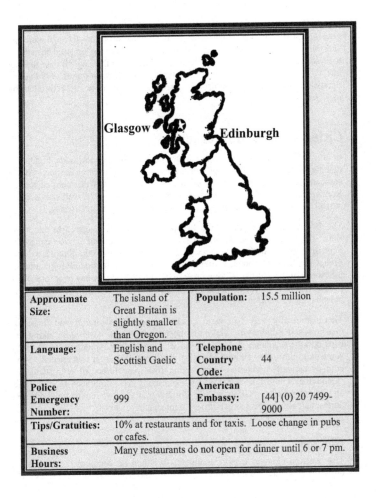

Approximate Size:	The island of Great Britain is slightly smaller than Oregon.	Population:	15.5 million
Language:	English and Scottish Gaelic	Telephone Country Code:	44
Police Emergency Number:	999	American Embassy:	[44] (0) 20 7499-9000
Tips/Gratuities:	10% at restaurants and for taxis. Loose change in pubs or cafes.		
Business Hours:	Many restaurants do not open for dinner until 6 or 7 pm.		

History and Overview:

Most people today picture Scottish men wearing kilts with beards and long hair. The stereotype is historically true of Scotland's early inhabitants. Present-day Scotland was once made up of warring tribes and different clans within those tribes. They were typically hairy, had painted faces, and carried primitive weapons. The tribes were proud people and determined not to be taken by the Romans. They fought back and were eventually separated from the Romans after the empire constructed Hadrian's Wall.

Long periods of being under English rule and standing alone made the Scottish government slightly weak. The crowns united under occasions through marriage and this produced a chain of Scottish-born leaders backing England instead of their native land. Scots tended to be seen as inferior to the English over its long history, and this resentment is still underlying today. It wasn't until 1999 that the Scottish Parliament was re-instated after 292 years of being controlled by members in London.

Cities/Points of Interest:

In Northern Britain lies the small country of Scotland. Its lowlands, highlands, mountains and lakes make it one of the most unique places in Europe. At the southern border of Scotland are remnants of Hadrian's Wall, constructed by Roman Emperor Hadrian to keep the "barbarians" at bay. The wall stands at the narrowest part of the island and can still be walked on by tourists today.

The British, although part of the European Union, never agreed to adopt the Euro. England uses the pound but the Scots use their own version called the Scottish pound. The Scots will accept English currency but the English will not accept the Scottish pound, another facet that mirrors the underlying supposed inferiority of the Scottish. I found it easier to just convert money over to Scottish pounds because there is less room to get cheated with the conversion rates between the two currencies.

There are really only two main cities that appeal to tourists and those are Glasgow and Edinburgh. The cities become the home base while taking day trips into the highlands and places like St. Andrews and Aberdeen. If you have some extra time, play a round of golf in the country where it was created. Some courses are still traditional, only letting men play (after all golf stands for "Gentlemen Only, Ladies Forbidden") but many have embraced modern times and allow women. Glasgow and Edinburgh have two completely different atmospheres and appeal to two different interests.

Glasgow

This western city has a more industrial feel than its counterpart. Streets are crowded with cute, old taxis and businessmen and women walking to work. The town has less tourist attractions and less places to let loose, in comparison to Edinburgh. This is not to say, though, that Glasgow is short on entertainment.

Grand pedestrian areas are filled with shops and countless bars and pubs. Many of the places are smaller and very crowded. Each pub has a different theme and drink specials offered. Look at the boards or menus outside to check the prices and live entertainment from place to place.

I never felt particularly un-safe in Glasgow but I was unfortunate enough to have both of my cameras stolen in one night. Professional thieves thrive in places like crowded bars to find unsuspecting targets. Keep belongings close to you at all times and don't trust anyone.

Edinburgh

This is the place to be in Scotland. Edinburgh is the city younger people go to and subsequently it has more to do and more to see. Dominating the city is Edinburgh Castle sitting high atop a hill in the center of town. Adorning the sides of the hill and the park at its base are hundreds of species of trees, flowers and sweeping fields of daffodils.

The street leading down from the castle to Holyrood House is called the Royal Mile. This stretch of pavement is consumed with tourists but is worth the crowd. Little shops, locals engaging in debates and eerie alleys leading back into a web of streets give the Royal Mile the character and a reputation that precedes it.

View of Old Town in Edinburgh, Scotland

Scotland, like in Ireland and England, has a city bus that leads all over town and has a guide narrating the sites. A pass can be purchased permitting you to get on and off the bus for the entire day at one flat fee. This pass not only helps you to get around the city but it is also very informative.

It is possible to roam the Edinburgh city streets for hours upon hours. After walking through the old part of town and then onto the new city, my friend and I stumbled upon a large hill called Calton Hill. Atop the mound, gaze down at the entire city of Edinburgh and the Queen's Official Scottish Residence, The Palace of Holyroodhouse. Calton Hill has some old ruins and few to no tourists. It is a great place to sit, reflect, relax or read before retuning to the busy streets down below.

No visit to Edinburgh is complete without experiencing the bar scene. Rose Street has dozens of pubs in just a few short blocks. The pubs vie for the visitors' attention by naming their bars names like *Filthy McNasty's* or *Dirty Dicks*. Many businesspeople attend the pubs after work, but the majority of the demographics are made up of younger, college-aged students.

From Edinburgh there are a number of tours delving into the countryside and highlands of Europe. I recommend Rabbies Trail Burners. The price included an eight-hour trip into the highlands and lowlands of Scotland and a stop at the famous Loch Ness.

Loch Ness

My guide was the quintessential Scot with his thick brogue and traditional kilt.

Donnie gave interesting facts about Scottish history and showed us the areas used in the filming of places like *Braveheart* and *Harry Potter*. The highlight of our trip was stopping at the edge of Loch Ness in hopes to find the Loch Ness

Monster, "Nessie." Unfortunately we did not find her, but there were boats equipped with sonar devices to help aid in the search.

Scotland is not a big country and can be tackled in only a few days. It is one of the places in Europe that I feel has withstood outside influences and remains closest to its culture.

National Holidays	
January 1	New Year's Day
January 2	Bank Holiday
March/April	Good Friday
March/April	Easter Monday
1st Monday in May	May Day
Last Monday in May	Spring Bank Holiday
1st Monday in August	Summer Bank Holiday
Last Monday of August	Summer Bank Holiday
December 25	Christmas Day
December 26	Boxing Day

Spain

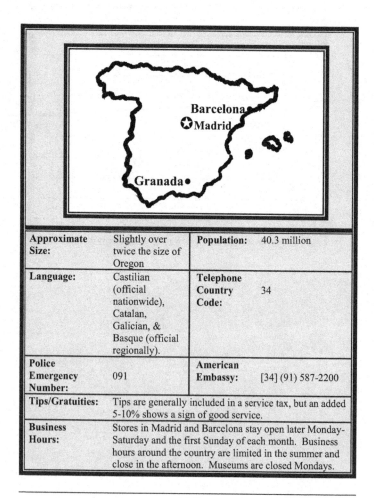

Approximate Size:	Slightly over twice the size of Oregon	Population:	40.3 million
Language:	Castilian (official nationwide), Catalan, Galician, & Basque (official regionally).	Telephone Country Code:	34
Police Emergency Number:	091	American Embassy:	[34] (91) 587-2200
Tips/Gratuities:	Tips are generally included in a service tax, but an added 5-10% shows a sign of good service.		
Business Hours:	Stores in Madrid and Barcelona stay open later Monday-Saturday and the first Sunday of each month. Business hours around the country are limited in the summer and close in the afternoon. Museums are closed Mondays.		

History and Overview:

Spain has a very old and nostalgic feel about it. The earliest signs of habitation date back to 15,000-12,000 b.c.e. when cave paintings were drawn and recently uncovered at Altamira. Ancient Rome conquered much of Spain and built aqueducts and camps as a place to hold their troops. The countryside appears to have been through a lot and the occasional Roman ruin will remind visitors of the long Spanish history.

In 711, the North African Moors, a Muslim people from present day Morocco, Algeria and Libya, invaded the Iberian Peninsula. The Islamic influence cannot be overlooked, especially in the southern towns like Granada. Huge buildings are constructed following Islamic architecture styles and principles. Alongside the architecture, influences from Arabic made its way into many words in the Spanish language.

After centuries of Moors existing in Spain, King Ferdinand and Isabella started up the Spanish Inquisition in 1492. This sought to oust all Jews, Moors, and Protestants from Spain. It was the same year Columbus was commissioned by Ferdinand and Isabella to discover a northern passage to Asia. Along the way, he stumbled onto North America. Not long after, the Spanish conquistadors moved to America to convert the locals and extract the resources.

A sudden influx of gold, silver, and other goods from the New World quickly caused serious inflation and made the economy collapse. With a failing economy and the defeat of the Spanish Armada, Spain lost much of the power it had gained during the Age of Exploration.

Cities/Points of Interest:

Spain is often a difficult country to make time to see, because it is not nestled neatly between the other tourist hotbeds of France, Germany, and Switzerland. South of the Pyrenees, bordered by Portugal on one side and water on the others, Spain is quite isolated. Its rich culture and tradition still remains very vibrant and vital in everyday life. Each area of Spain is unique from the next, but there is still a definite link between each province to make them all Spanish in nature.

Madrid

Resting in the center of the country and acting as the governmental capital, Madrid provides all the perks of a European capital city. Its palace is one of the best in Europe and can compete arm in arm with any of the more famous ones of France, Germany, and Austria. Within walking distance is the Plaza Mayor. This city square is the hub for tour groups and outdoor cafes. You can enjoy tapas while gazing at the many different façades, colors and time periods making up the magnificent square.

The city is fairly large but many of the scenic areas in town are in relative close proximity and can be easily handled by foot. Acquaint yourself with the map of

Plaza Mayor

Madrid, and be willing to get lost in its backstreets and city squares. The Puerta del Sol marks the center of town, and from there, you can feel free to explore all of its arms, pointing in different directions of town.

The elegance and relative calm of Madrid is a great starting off point. After becoming familiar with Spain and its people, a trip to Barcelona is suggested for the more adventurous traveler.

Barcelona

Barcelona is by far one of the most interesting and unique cities in Europe. Architecture from Antoni Gaudí dots the town and his modernist buildings are everywhere. The buildings seem to fit in perfectly with the colorful and extroverted Barcelonan atmosphere. Barcelona is the capital city of the autonomous region of Catalon. This eastern area of Spain has its own language and culture, distinct from the rest of the country. Catalon's mixing of cultures and languages make it a very diverse area open to accepting different backgrounds.

Barcelona can feel large at times, but utilizing the public transportation and having an idea of what you want to see before you start meandering the streets, can keep walking and confusion to a minimum.

There are few key areas to spend the majority of your time: la Rambla, l'Eixample, and Montjuïc.

Start off by walking La Rambla. It is Barcelona's most famous street and it leads from the waterfront down a promenade lined with trees and facades. This area has most of the historical sites and places of interest for tourists.

Another area to consider visiting is into l'Eixample. This newer section of Barcelona has many examples of Gaudí's modern architecture. His buildings never have straight lines or sharp corners. The colors and styles of Gaudí are truly unique and not to be missed. L'Eixample also has an expansive commercial district to act as a diversion from the often-exhausting site seeing. Take a break in one of the many restaurants or pop in and out of small shops while taking in the younger part of Barcelona.

Finally, for a more relaxing excursion, climb atop the hill dominating Barcelona to the south, Montjuïc. After resting up in the recreational park or having a picnic, reflect on Barcelona from the view at the top of the hill. The panorama is beautiful and peaceful. Nearby, for a change of pace and a bit more modern feel, visit the Olympic Park just southeast of Montjuïc to visit the home of the 1992 summer games.

Andalusia

Quickly becoming one of the most popular tourist destinations for Europeans, Andalusia has a lot to offer and never fails to present its visitors with gorgeous weather and even better day trips. Dominated by the city of Seville, southern Spain has many spectacular smaller cities to visit. No less important and sometimes more rewarding than the big cities, towns like Córdoba, Granada, and Ronda will definitely not disappoint. Córdoba feels more like a city with its large shopping malls and business buildings. Granada and Ronda are very different in comparison. Granada houses the Alhambra, a Moorish Palace, as well as some other exceptional tourist destinations, while Ronda is a quieter old town with a magnificent gorge and the oldest bull ring in Spain.

The Alhambra, Granada

Take a full day trip down to the British owned area of Gibraltar, then catch a ferry over to Africa and experience the Islamic country of Morocco. You leave the monkey inhabited Rock of Gibraltar for the chaotic and bustling Medina of Tangier. For many who don't have the intention or the finances to accommodate a trip to Africa, the touristy town of Tangier is the closest way to experience the "forgotten continent." Prepare yourself for crowds and the sometimes over-performed tourist shows. Take it for what it's worth and look to the less crowded streets with every day people and every day life; this is what Morocco is meant to be. Generally, I prefer to stay away from guided tours, but Tangier is one destination that I would highly recommend taking one. The language barrier and culture clash may be too much to handle for first-time travelers.

Andalusia could occupy an entire vacation if given the time. This is an area to rent a car or splurge to buy guided group tours. Explore the lesser-known towns and sunbathe on the magnificent gold coast.

For ways to experience traditional Spanish culture munch on some tapas (appetizers) during the early evening at a tapa bar. Dinner does not begin for most Spaniards until 9 or 10. Curb your appetite by feasting on the Spanish tapas and then grab a meal later to dine with the locals.

Some evenings should be set aside for a bullfight. Be warned that in Spain, the bull does not have a happy ending. During the three-act engagement, the bull gets weakened and eventually killed by the matador. To see a less gruesome bull fight, those in France spare the bull. However, no Spanish trip is complete without visiting a bullring or an actual bullfight.

Whether visiting subdued Madrid, eccentric Barcelona or gorgeous Andalusia, Spain has so much to offer. The olive groves litter the countryside. The sandy beaches form its boundaries. The towns give it character. Spain offers many different vacations in one. The question is: which one do you want to take?

National Holidays	
January 1	New Year's Day
January 6	Epiphany
March 19	St. Joseph's Day
March/April	Good Friday
March/April	Easter Monday
May 1	Labor Day
May/June	Pentecost Monday
June 24	St. John's Day
August 15	Assumption of the Virgin
September 11	National Day (Catalonia)
September 24	Our Lady of Mercy Day
October 12	National Day
November 1	All Saints' Day
December 6	Constitution Day
December 8	Immaculate Conception
December 25	Christmas Day
December 26	St. Stephen's Day

Sweden

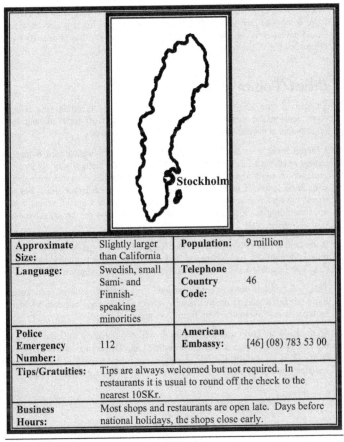

Approximate Size:	Slightly larger than California	**Population:**	9 million
Language:	Swedish, small Sami- and Finnish-speaking minorities	**Telephone Country Code:**	46
Police Emergency Number:	112	**American Embassy:**	[46] (08) 783 53 00
Tips/Gratuities:	Tips are always welcomed but not required. In restaurants it is usual to round off the check to the nearest 10SKr.		
Business Hours:	Most shops and restaurants are open late. Days before national holidays, the shops close early.		

History and Overview:

Once completely covered by ice sheets, Sweden began to see a change in lifestyles as the ice receded and hunter-gatherers moved in. The Sami (or Lapps) are believed to be decedents of these primitive people and still live in the far north of Sweden. In 1989, the Sami people were granted their own parliament.

Like in other Scandinavian histories, the Vikings played an important role. This time period brought wealth and more people to the area, eventually settling down and living the Scandinavian way of life.

The Union of Kalmar united Denmark, Sweden, and Norway causing yet another tie between the nations. Following suit after its counterparts, Sweden also converted to Lutheran Protestantism in 1523.

The Swedish are a relaxed and quiet people. Most of this is attributed to the large amount of land for the limited amount of people, but it is also because the Scandinavian way of life is slower-paced and less confrontational that many other societies in Europe.

Cities/Points of Interest:

Sweden is the largest and most visited of the Scandinavian countries. Apprehensions of weather and distance tend to put off travelers, but in my opinion that is the reason to visit this enchanting country.

I toured Sweden at the beginning of February and it was indeed colder than almost anything I have experienced. With this cold though, was obviously the presence of snow and ice. The inlets and other bodies of water were guarded with thick sheets of ice and snow banks piling high on either side. For me, I would have been disappointed to see Sweden any other way. I merely bundled up, resembling the kid from *A Christmas Story* and set out on my adventure to take in Sweden.

If the cold is not for you, the summer temperatures can get as high as the upper 60's. Regardless, the crispness and purity of the air makes any weather condition bearable and the daily excursions around the country worth it.

There are multiple ways to enter Sweden. I opted for the extremely inexpensive Ryan Air flight landing me in a nearby suburb. Other ways to get to Sweden are by ferry from Finland or a train from Denmark or Norway.

Most of my attention was focused on Stockholm, but for a long day trip I took the five-hour train ride across the Swedish Lake District to visit Norway. This train ride is fully worth the fare if you do not intend to visit or have the means necessary to explore other areas of Sweden. The views are breathtaking.

Stockholm

Built on over a dozen islands, Stockholm is a beautiful city with its old and new districts, as well as an abundance of waterways dividing neighborhoods.

Gamla Stan is the most popular destination because it is the center of old Stockholm. You can look at aged buildings and begin to understand the Swedish way of life and culture. Surrounding Gamla Stan and other islands are a series of botels which are essentially boats made into hotels that rest on the water. For the price of a nice hostel, you can mingle with other tourists, look out the portholes

Gamla Stan with botels in water.

to see Stockholm, and fall asleep to the swaying water of the inlets. This was an adorable way to spend our nights in Stockholm and to break away from the norms of hotels and other unauthentic feeling hostels.

After visiting the old district in Gamla Stan, a walk to the royal palace is in order. Known as Kungliga Slottet, the Royal Palace also practices the changing of the guard everyday at noon. Nearly all of the royal palaces in Europe perform this tradition, but the lack of crowds and barriers between viewers and the guards made this moment more intimate than the famed presentation in London. The show lasts about fifteen minutes and is quite entertaining.

The city can feel large, so at times it may be wise to take advantage of the public bus system organized throughout Stockholm. Cabs can be expensive and the subway can be confusing. Board one of the inexpensive buses and ride around town. Jump off at whatever place seems appealing. If time permits, get off at one of the many museums in Stockholm. All are noteworthy, but my personal

favorite was the Vasamuseet. This enclosure houses the 18th century sailing ship, the *Vasa* which sank and killed thousands of men. The difference in nature and style of this museum compared to the typical ones housing paintings and sculptures is interesting even to those who know little about the *Vasa*.

Stockholm's commercial district is immense and extremely crowded. In the district of Norrmalm, there are hundreds of shops, malls, restaurants and many more people. Merchandise can be expensive, but the selection and variety is enormous.

After taking advantage of the sites, people, and shopping in Stockholm, be daring and try the local specialty, reindeer, which is on many of the menus.   Although reindeer may not be your first choice of a delicacy, always try to be open to new cultures. It will be that reindeer in Stockholm not the McDonald's that will be the most memorable.

Sweden's Lake District at sunset

National Holidays	
January 1	New Year's Day
January 6	Epiphany
March/April	Good Friday
March/April	Easter Monday
May	Ascension Day
May 1	Labor Day
May/June	Pentecost Monday
June (Saturday nearest June 21)	Midsummer's Day
November 1	All Saints' Day
November 11	Armistice Day
December 25	Christmas Day
December 26	St. Stephen's Day

Switzerland

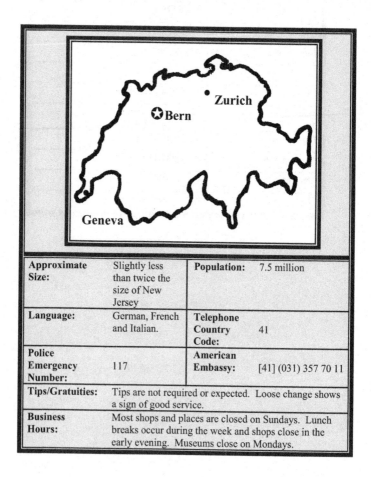

Approximate Size:	Slightly less than twice the size of New Jersey	Population:	7.5 million
Language:	German, French and Italian.	Telephone Country Code:	41
Police Emergency Number:	117	American Embassy:	[41] (031) 357 70 11
Tips/Gratuities:	Tips are not required or expected. Loose change shows a sign of good service.		
Business Hours:	Most shops and places are closed on Sundays. Lunch breaks occur during the week and shops close in the early evening. Museums close on Mondays.		

History and Overview:

Located directly north of present-day Italy, it wa
to the once powerful Holy Roman Empire
Peninsula. The native tribes were incorporate
overly hostile with the invaders. After the Ro
Burghundians occupied the western region, stil
Germanic Alemains settled in the North and Ea
Over its history Switzerland was occupied
speaking different languages. Today the country is still split with three national
languages, along the same regions divided nearly 1,600 years ago.

John Calvin started up his Reformation movement in Geneva. His words
connected with many of the Swiss, showing why some of the country became
Protestant while others remained Catholic.

1648 was an important year for Switzerland because the Treaty of Westphalia
recognized Swiss neutrality and the independence of its thirteen cantons. Then
and still today, Switzerland is a neutral state and runs as a confederation. Each
canton runs separately under the greater laws of Switzerland.

The peaceful Swiss have managed to become one of the only two nations in the
world to be neutral in any conflict. This neutrality shows through in the people
and the daily life. The Swiss have embraced their multi-cultural, multi-lingual
heritage. The people are accepting, kind, and efficient. This harmony makes
Switzerland a fantastic place to visit; everything seems to run perfectly, on time
and in a hospitable manner.

Cities/Points of Interest:

Located at the center of Europe and home to the largest mountain peaks on the
continent, Switzerland has always been an important vacation destination for
Europeans and Americans alike. Its abundance of hiking trails and skiing has
given Switzerland an influx of nature lovers and adrenaline seekers.

Bern, Swtizerland

The Swiss are a very
tolerant and polite
people. The division of
two major religions,
three national
languages, and twenty-
six separate cantons
has made Switzerland
very well-rounded and
accepting. It is
extremely easy to find
English speakers and
everything seems to be
running with the

...ness of the French and the efficiency of the Germans. Switzerland has ...n on many different influences, but has emerged distinctly Swiss.

Although very expensive and usually catering to the outdoorsman, Switzerland can be very enjoyable to see. If you are not into hiking or skiing, you might want to consider less time in this central European country. The cities in Switzerland are not as dense with historical sites and landmarks as many of the other cities in Europe. Use your time in Switzerland to regroup before moving onto another place.

Geneva and Zurich

I lump these two major Swiss cities together because they basically have the same things to offer. Both Geneva and Zurich are perched along a pristine lake with low-story buildings. Venture into the old towns and visit St. Peter's Church (Yes, each city has one) and educate yourself in one of the many museums in either city.

Don't forget to take in what the Swiss are best known for…chocolate. Dive into a box of decadent sweets, or feel free to go another route and try one of the hundreds of different cheeses made and distributed in the country. While dining in Switzerland it is not necessary to tip the server, a service charge is already included in the price of the meal. Gratuities vary from country to country so take a glance at the check to see if it already has a V.A.S.T (value added sales tax) or a service tax calculated in.

Swiss Countryside

When thinking of Switzerland, most think of the Alps or sprawling meadows filled with cows interrupted by a stream or lake. This precise vision is why I

traveled to Switzerland. The best areas for seeing the mountains, lakes and meadows are in the center of the country around the towns of Interlaken, Grindelwald, and Mürren. These towns are all close in proximity and due to the number of tourists, caters to visitors.

Upon arriving into a town visit the local tourist office for timetables of lifts, trains, and other activities in the area. To reach the high country, it might be wise to purchase lift tickets. Rather than hiking a strenuous uphill climb, lift tickets are a cheap and quick way to reach the towns in the mountains. The same goes for anywhere. If you know you will be returning to your original destination purchase round-trip tickets, this not only saves money but also saves you the time of waiting in line for a second go. Roundtrips are always cheaper and always easier than buying two one-way tickets.

If you are looking to escape the crowds, however, these three towns are not the places to go. Especially in Interlaken and Grindelwald, they have especially become over-run with tourists. To stay comfortably in a town with English speakers and tourist activities these are good places to visit for first time travelers. If you are adventurous and open to the possibility of limited English speakers and deluxe accommodations, venture farther into the countryside and away from what you can find in some of the busiest cities in Europe.

Switzerland is a hiker's paradise and the site of the Alps cannot be matched anywhere else in Europe. To get away from the cities and other tourists lose yourself in the Swiss countryside. A reliable train and a smiling face are never too far away. If you are to get lost anywhere, Switzerland is the place to do it.

National Holidays	
January 1	New Year's Day
March/April	Good Friday
March/April	Easter Monday
May	Ascension Day
May/June	Pentecost Monday
August 1	National Day
December 25	Christmas Day
December 26	St. Stephen's Day

Cited Sources:

www.xc.com

www.state.gov

The Guide to Premier Destinations, AAA Europe Travel Book. AAA
Publishing: Heathrow. 6th Edition, 2004.

Rick Steves

www.abacci.com

www.britannia.com

www.rootsweb.com

www.cia.gov

geography.about.com

www.lib.utexas.edu/maps/europe

CPSIA information can be obtained
at www.ICGtesting.com
Printed in the USA
BVOW03s1949181217
503136BV00001B/16/P